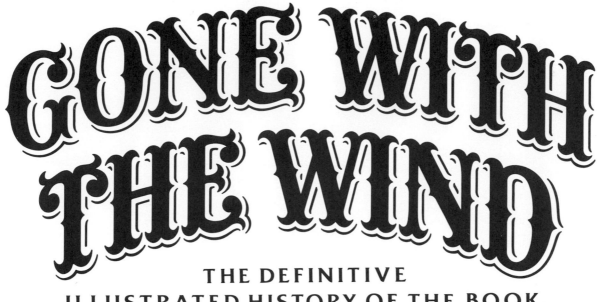

GONE WITH THE WIND

THE DEFINITIVE ILLUSTRATED HISTORY OF THE BOOK, THE MOVIE, AND THE LEGEND

BY HERB BRIDGES
AND TERRYL C. BOODMAN

SIMON & SCHUSTER

LONDON • SYDNEY • NEW YORK • TOKYO • TORONTO

First published in Great Britain by
Simon & Schuster Ltd in 1989

Copyright © Herb Bridges, 1989
Published by arrangement with Turner Entertainment Co.
GONE WITH THE WIND
© 1939 Selznick, Ren. 1967 Metro-Goldwyn-Mayer
© 1989 Turner Entertainment Co. All rights reserved.

Simon & Schuster Ltd
West Garden Place
Kendal Street
London W2 2AP.

Simon & Schuster of Australia Pty Ltd
Sydney

British Library Cataloguing-in-Publication Data Available
ISBN 0-671-69695-5

Cover and interior designed by
Michaelis/Carpelis Design Associates, Inc.

A book from Puck Productions

Printed and bound in Great Britain by
Richard Clay Ltd, Bungay, Suffolk

2 4 6 8 10 9 7 5 3 1

For fans of GWTW everywhere and in every time.
Herb Bridges

For my family, from whom *I* draw my strength.
Terryl C. Boodman

CONTENTS

INTRODUCTION

December 15, 1939: the opening night of *Gone With the Wind*, a long awaited, much anticipated movie event throughout the country and around the world. As the lights dimmed, the curtains rose and the film burst into Technicolor, Rhett and Scarlett, Melanie and Ashley, Tara and Civil War Atlanta came to life. From that very first night, their loves, losses, and passions burned deep in the hearts of moviegoers.

December 1989 marks the 50th Anniversary of the premiere of *Gone With the Wind*. Time has not dimmed its impact on the popular culture of the world. The movie's prismatic costumes and sets, spectacular sunsets and soaring music are as thrilling today as they were half a century earlier.

This book has been designed to give you the story behind the legend—from Margaret Mitchell's award-winning novel to casting to location shooting to pre- and post-production to the original premieres to critics' reviews and re-releases. It is the story of a "land of Cavaliers and Cotton Fields called the Old South . . ."

CHAPTER ONE

The LEGEND

THE LEGEND

*I*n the spring of 1936, a new novel blew onto the American scene with the force of a hurricane—*Gone With the Wind*. Essentially the story of a willful girl and the people around her during and after the Civil War, the book was an overnight sensation, selling a million copies and commanding thirty-one printings in its first year of publication.

People were crazy about *GWTW*, as it soon became known. The first printing sold out almost as fast as it rolled off the presses. Eager fans thronged around its author each time she set foot on a city street, as if she were a movie star, while the press beat a path to her door and never left it. *GWTW* had arrived.

Now, more than fifty years later, it is still popular. Readers are just as apt now, as then, to discover it sold out in bookstores and already checked out in libraries.

What was the mind behind *Gone With the Wind?* How was a work of such enduring popularity created? To know that, one must know its author, Margaret Mitchell. And to know her, one must slip back in time.

Atlanta, Georgia, 1900. The War Between the States had been waged and lost only thirty-five years earlier and was still a fresh and vivid memory. In the gracious homes that lined Peachtree Street and the shanties along Decatur Street still lived the survivors of a conflict that had already taken permanent root in the collective consciousness of the South and flourished.

Margaret Munnerlyn Mitchell was born on November 8 of that year, the fifth generation of her family to proudly call themselves Atlantans, steeped in the legends of the city and the South.

As a child she spent long, lazy Sunday afternoons "sitting on the bony knees of Confederate veterans and the fat, slick laps of old ladies who had survived the war," listening to tales of relatives who walked fifty miles with their skulls cracked by Yankee bullets, stuffed wrapping paper beneath their corsets to keep warm during the blockade, and sat down to supper with Rebel leaders. And all these tales were told not as epic drama but as ordinary family happenings that could have occurred just yesterday.

When she was six, Margaret herself became a rebel, against going to school. On a blazing hot September day her mother drove her out along the road to Jonesboro, pointing out the ruins of great houses that had fallen during or because of the war, chimneys standing ghostly among the scattered leaves and creeping foliage of the encroaching woods. She also pointed out the proud homes that still stood, testimony to their owners' steely spirit.

She explained that all the people who had once lived in all the houses had believed they had wealth and beauty and good times that would never end. But their world did end. And it would happen again, Margaret's mother warned. And when it did, she had better be prepared. "...All that would be left after a world ended would be what you could do with your hands and what you had in your head," not the least of which was an education. Margaret went to school.

Margaret grew up with the twentieth century, a Jazz Age baby, sufficiently enlightened in the New Era of women's equality to set off for college with aspirations of becoming a neurologist or psychiatrist. During her first year, however, her mother died in the influenza epidemic of 1919, and she came home to keep house for her father and brother.

A freethinking flapper, "one of those short-haired, short-skirted, hard-boiled young women who preachers said would go to hell or be hanged before they were thirty," as she described herself, Margaret talked her way into, and succeeded admirably at, a position as a reporter for the *Atlanta Journal Sunday Magazine*, no mean

Margaret and her father, Eugene, peruse a copy of *Gone With the Wind* at the family home in 1936.

feat in an age where the only newspapermen were men.

Margaret—Peggy, her friends called her—moved about in a modern world of moving pictures, speedy automobiles, electric iceboxes, airplanes, and radios, but to her the Civil War was just as recent and probably more real.

She found herself in 1926, at the height of the Jazz Age, housebound with a broken ankle that developed into arthritis she began to write a novel about the Civil War.

She was first of all a voracious reader. Her husband, John Marsh, brought home armloads of library books every night to entertain her until one evening he announced that he had exhausted the supply; she had read every book in the library except the exact sciences. Dropping a sheaf of copy paper in her lap, he told her she now had no choice but to write her own book.

She didn't know why she chose the Civil War as her subject, she would later say; it was just always there in her background.

The first chapter she wrote was the final one, in which Rhett leaves Scarlett alone to think about him "tomorrow," and from there she wrote a chapter here and a chapter there, apparently in no particular sequence, but as the spirit moved her. As each chapter was completed, it was sealed into a manila envelope and stacked next to the typewriter. When the stack became two and the two became towers, the envelopes were squirreled away in varying spots in the three-room apartment—some under the bed, some under the sofa, others in the pots-and-pans cupboard.

When friends visited, the typewriter and the current chapter were covered over with a large bath towel. Peggy didn't like people to know she was working on a book. And, anyway, she never planned to sell it; it was only for her own amusement.

Sometime in 1929, the novel was finished, all except for the opening chapter and two others. The stock market crashed, a black and ominous Depression fell over the world, and Margaret Mitchell went on about the business of being Mrs. Peggy Marsh.

She had written the book mostly during the three years she had spent laid up, sometimes bedridden, with her bad ankle, having been told by doctors that she might never walk again. She finished the book, her ankle thankfully healed, and as she put it, "When my foot got well, I stopped writing because walking seemed far more interesting."

Peggy had been engaged once, to a young man who was shortly thereafter killed in World War I, and married once before—for a period of only months—to a fellow emotionally unequipped for life with the headstrong Margaret. But now her ship had come in.

Being Mrs. Marsh was fun. Peggy and John lived in a small, dark apartment they affectionately called "The Dump" and used as a base for lively, intellectually stimulating dinner parties and evening entertainments. Life flowed on like Southern molasses, sometimes thick and grainy, crystallized with illnesses or the woes of friends, but always sweet.

Then, in the spring of 1935, life abruptly changed.

Lois Cole, one of the few intimates who knew Peggy had been writing a book, was working for the Macmillan Company, publishers, in New York. The firm had reasoned that Southern books by new authors were frequent sellers and decided to send senior editor Harold Latham on a tour of the South. Lois suggested that he stop and talk with Peggy Marsh. Mr. Latham followed through, calling on her at her home.

Mrs. Marsh, however, insisted that she was not an author, was not writing, had never written a book, and wasn't the least bit interested in being reviewed by any publisher. Mr. Latham packed his bags and prepared to leave Atlanta.

But first he attended a tea where Peggy introduced him to a young girl who did hope to make it big as an author. As she drove the girl and her friends home from the tea, another young lady in the car spilled the beans about Peggy writing a book. The first girl was amazed. She couldn't believe that Mrs. Marsh could write. She didn't seem the type. She took life much too lightly, the girl said, and was wasting her time trying to be a serious novelist. As Peggy put it later, the girl had said, "And you've never even been refused by a publisher? I've been refused by the very best...."

That was it. Peggy rushed home, gathered up all the manila envelopes from all their hiding places—except the ones under the bed and in the pots-and-pans closet, which she forgot—rushed down to the hotel with them, and thrust them at the unsuspecting Mr. Latham. "My idea," she said, "was that at least I could brag that I had been refused by the very best publisher."

The envelopes were so unwieldy and so

voluminous that Mr. Latham, who had been half out the door to catch the next train, was forced first to go into town and buy a new suitcase to carry his newly acquired manuscript.

At the moment that Harold Latham safely left Atlanta, Peggy came to her senses. She realized what she had let out of her grasp and was "appalled." Desperately she wired ahead to Mr. Latham's next hotel, requesting that he send back the offending, "sloppy" manuscript. But Harold Latham had already begun reading the book and had fallen under its spell. Instead of sending it back, he offered to buy it.

Back in New York, Peggy's untitled novel wove its magic around the entire Macmillan Company, and the firm set a publication date for May 1936. That left the author only six months to complete the still unwritten opening chapter, two other bridging chapters, perform the numerous revisions she felt necessary, and fact-check the entire manuscript—a bow to historical accuracy she insisted on.

Peggy Marsh was now Margaret Mitchell again—at least as far as the novel was concerned—and it seemed to consume her entire life. Working up to twenty hours a day in a feverish rush to meet the publisher's deadline, always terrified that some historical fact would escape her strict attention, she devoted all her waking and sleeping hours to the book.

Her husband, John, who had been a copy editor when they met, proofed every page. Her father, Eugene Mitchell, an expert on the history of the period, acted as consultant. With their assistance the book was finally completed in January 1936.

It still had no title. Macmillan was sending it to press with a working title, *Tomorrow Is Another Day*, when Margaret sent them a list of dozens of possible alternatives, including her favorite, *Gone with the Wind*.

She had found the phrase in "Cynara," a poem by Ernest Dowson. She chose the line because, she said, "it had the far away, faintly sad sound I wanted." The Macmil-

lan people agreed, and the book sailed off to press, named at last.

Gone with the Wind (yes, the word *with* started out with a lowercase *w*) rolled off the presses in May 1936 as planned. The official publication date, however—meaning the date advertising and reviews would commence—was postponed a month until June, because the Book of the Month Club had chosen it as its July featured selection.

But advance word on *GWTW* spread like wildfire, and by June 30, the official release date, bookstores were already placing frantic reorders. Libraries tried futilely to fill requests for the book. Friends fervently urged dog-eared copies on friends. In fact, by June 30, the first printing of ten thousand copies had been swept away on a tide of excitement and almost one hundred thousand copies were being shipped around the country.

Margaret Mitchell was miserable. She had adored the quiet, unassuming life of Peggy Marsh. Now, as a famous authoress, her phone never stopped ringing, her doorbell never stopped shrilling; she could scarcely walk down a city street without being accosted by well-wishers, autograph hounds, reporters anxious for an interview. Strangers demanded to know if Scarlett ever got Rhett back and insisted she write a sequel so they could find out. Ladies' club members requested that she speak at their meetings, and on and on....

Margaret fled to the mountains, someplace quiet without telephones or telegrams, someplace where she could at least sit down in peace and read her reviews.

These thrilled her. She had never considered herself more than a passable writer ("lousy" is the way she once put it) and she was delighted at how favorable the reviews were.

She was also too much of a lady not to thank each of her reviewers and as many of the well-wishers who wrote her as possible. Before, during, and after her week-long sojourn in the hills, Margaret personally wrote each of these people charming, witty, lengthy letters and only increased the exhaustion she had brought upon herself racing to meet her manuscript deadline. Finally her eyes rebelled with an attack of severe strain, forcing the rest of her diminutive body to follow them into a darkened room to lie quietly beneath black bandages and only *dictate* thank-you letters for months.

People still frequently asked, was there a real Tara? A real Twelve Oaks? A real Rhett? Or Scarlett? Or Ashley? Did she plan for her novel to mirror the Great Depression?

Margaret insisted that her characters were real, not as specific individuals—she strove mightily to avoid that—but as types; people she had known all her life. They were different than those romantic-novel "lavender-and-lace-moonlight-on-the-magnolias people," she said. They were "remarkably tough...they had to be...or they'd never have survived."

She had researched for years the way people lived during the war, how they dressed, what they looked like—again, for her own amusement. For example, she described Rhett Butler as looking the way he did because he was "typical of his times.... I went through hundreds of old ambrotypes and daguerreotypes looking at faces, and that type of face leaped out at you." Not to mention the fact that Rhett's was the type that seemed to have lingered the longest in the minds and hearts of the elderly ladies she slyly interviewed about their old beaux.

Margaret steadfastly maintained that there was no *real* Tara, though people frequently refused to believe her. She had invented it and Twelve Oaks out of whole cloth. But, like everything and everyone else in the book, she had so meticulously researched both landscape and architecture that only a slight wave of the hand of fate must have prevented their actual existence.

As for mirroring the Depression, Margaret insisted she never had any intention of doing so, and pointed out that when she began *GWTW*, the carefree, richly lived Jazz Age was at its peak. She had had no idea the Depression was on the horizon. She wrote about hard times, she said, because they were the stuff that was described to her throughout her childhood. They were the canvas on which her family's colorful heritage was painted.

People asked, and still ask, what gave the book its universal appeal. Perhaps this is the answer: She wrote about real people in real situations and made them live. She gave readers characters they could care about as much as they did themselves and their loved ones. And more than any other, there was the character of Scarlett, who determined that no matter what tragedies befell her—death or war or poverty—she would triumph, and not the situation. Scarlett was a survivor and a winner, to whom people of all ages, eras, and walks of life seemed able to relate.

All the events that occurred in the book had their basis in fact. They didn't all happen to the same people, or in the same time or place, but they all happened within the context of the war and Reconstruction. The only real difference between the events on paper and in history, Margaret said, was that she had had to water the more horrible ones down. They were too strong to be swallowed whole.

Horrible or not, Margaret's characters went on loving, living, and, in some cases, dying, and people everywhere followed along just as passionately as if they were bound up within the pages themselves.

Then David O. Selznick bought the movie rights for fifty thousand dollars. Margaret warned him that it would do him no good. She argued that the book was unfilmable and would cause him no end of headaches trying to *make* it a movie. But if he wanted the headache, he could have it.

He wanted it.

Margaret Mitchell stayed in Atlanta, trying hard to slip back into the simple life of Peggy Marsh, while David O. Selznick movie mogul, laid the plans to put *GWTW* on the silver screen.

CHAPTER TWO

Pre-
PRODUCTION

*G*one With the Wind was not David Selznick's discovery. It was first brought to his attention by Katharine Brown, the head of his New York story office. Macmillan had sent advance copies of the novel to leading movie studios, including Selznick International Pictures. After reading it Katharine immediately cabled to Selznick in Hollywood, saying: "I beg, urge, coax, and plead with you to read it at once.... I know that after you do you will drop everything and buy it."

David was not immediately sold on the idea. Common knowledge among studio executives held that Civil War pictures never made money. Selznick said that he might be more interested in *GWTW* if he had a female star to put in the lead, but since he didn't, he was turning it down.

Kay Brown refused to give up. She not only flooded Selznick with wires and memos on the book's possibilities but sent a copy to Jock Whitney, a principal backer of the studio, who immediately fell under its spell. Then, through either the magic of the book or the continued prodding of Brown and Whitney, Selznick decided to re-read the synopsis Kay had sent and changed his mind. On July 30, 1936, Selznick International and Margaret Mitchell signed the sale contract, providing the Atlanta lady with a tremendous sum of money for a first-time author and the fledgling studio (this would be only its eighth production) with an enormous financial risk.

The first thing David Selznick did with his new acquisition was to take it on a (Continued on page 16)

Facing page. A wardrobe still of Vivien Leigh in the white dress.

Tara, home of the O'Hara family. Located in fiction about 17 miles south of Altanta, it stood in fact on Forty Acres, the back lot of Selznick International Pictures and was more indicative of Hollywood's idea of the Old South than of the "healthy, hardy country and somewhat crude civilization" found in the novel. Note the guy-wired tree in the foreground.

Director George Cukor and set designer Hobe Erwin research local color on the balcony of an apartment facing Jackson Square in New Orleans. The year— 1937.

Actress Bebe Anderson (she later changed her name to Mary), raises the Confederate flag on the lawn of Selzick International to hail the start of filming on *Gone With the Wind.*

David O. Selznick, Vivien Leigh, Leslie Howard, and Olivia de Havilland sign the film contracts. The actors sent wires to Margaret Mitchell. Vivien's read: "...I pledge with all my heart I shall try to make Scarlett O'Hara live as you described her in your brilliant book." Olivia's said: "...to play Melanie means a long cherished dream realized;" and Leslie Howard sent this: "I am not at all envious of Rhett because thanks to you, it was Melanie, ma'am, that I wanted."

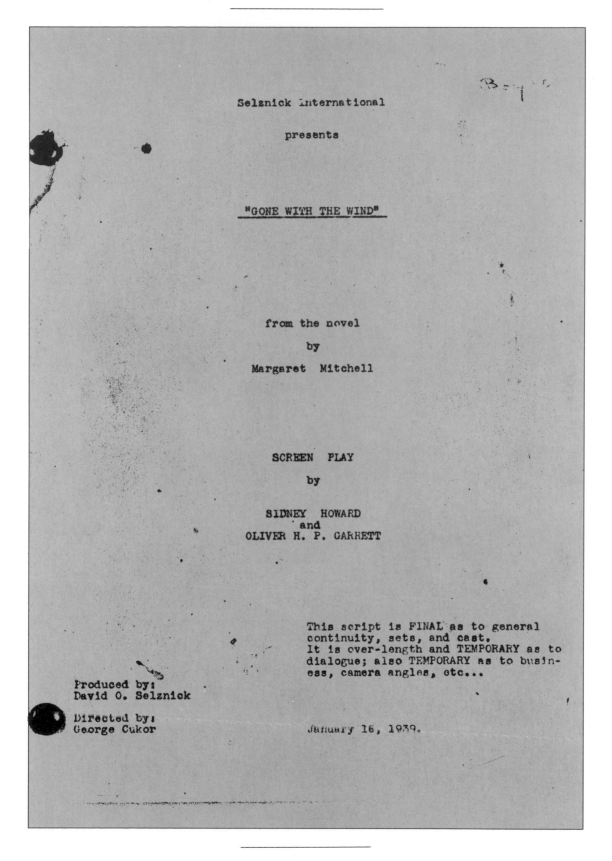

Selznick International

presents

"GONE WITH THE WIND"

from the novel

by

Margaret Mitchell

SCREEN PLAY

by

SIDNEY HOWARD
and
OLIVER H. P. GARRETT

This script is FINAL as to general
continuity, sets, and cast.
It is over-length and TEMPORARY as to
dialogue; also TEMPORARY as to business, camera angles, etc...

Produced by:
David O. Selznick

Directed by:
George Cukor

January 16, 1939.

Clark Gable
as Rhett
Butler.

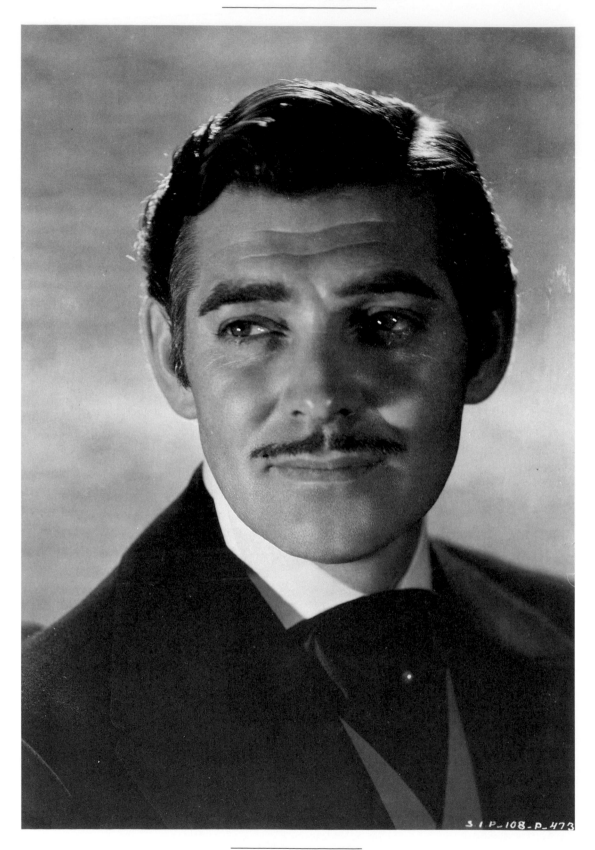

PRE-PRODUCTION

(Continued from page 9)
cruise to Hawaii to get better acquainted with it. He had read only the synopsis, so under tropical sunsets, he carefully read through the book, scribbling copious notes in the margins.

Selznick was no novice when it came to movie adaptations of famous books. He had already produced *David Copperfield, A Tale of Two Cities,* and *The Prisoner of Zenda*—the last two starring dashing, pencil-mustached Ronald Colman. All had been popular and critical successes. David knew how to please an audience and was committed to remaining faithful to the original work—changing as little of the story as possible—and casting to type.

Now, all he had to do was figure out how to condense the mammoth length of *GWTW* into an average ninety-minute movie, and who to put in the lead roles.

By the time he returned from Hawaii, everyone else in the country was reading *Gone With the Wind* as well. It seemed that every one of the millions of readers who had already devoured it knew who would make the perfect Rhett and the ideal Scarlett, and that they were all sending their suggestions to David Selznick.

Letters poured into the studio from every quarter, Housewives, ladies' clubs, newspaper columnists, radio commentators, magazine writers, and moviegoers at large deluged Selznick with fervent casting requests.

Rhett Butler was easy. According to a studio poll, 98% of the people who wrote in saw Clark Gable as the devilish blockade runner. Although Gary Cooper and Ronald Colman had their supporters, from the outset the part seemed tailor-made for Gable.

But Gable was not the least bit interested in playing Rhett Butler. In fact, he was completely opposed to the idea. He feared that it would be impossible to deliver in one character the romantic hero so many readers had magnified a thousandfold, in a thousand different ways, in their own minds.

"It wasn't that I didn't appreciate the compliment the public was paying me," he

Susan Myrick, technical adviser, and Evelyn Keyes (Scarlett's sister, Suellen) study the script on Tara's broad lawn.

said. "It was simply that Rhett was too big an order. I didn't want any part of him.... Rhett was too much for any actor to tackle in his right mind."

But Gable was lucky. He had an escape. He was under contract to MGM, and Louis B. Mayer, head of MGM and Selznick's father-in-law, would not let him out of it to make money for somebody else, even if it was his daughter's husband.

In the meantime the public, having settled on the casting of Rhett for itself, went on to Scarlett. And in this case, all of America had a different candidate in mind. So did every starlet and actress in Hollywood—namely herself. Everyone from Lucille Ball to Jean Arthur to Joan Crawford tested for the part. At various times Selznick seriously considered Taullulah Bankhead, Norma Shearer, and Paulette Goddard. But none fit the role. Out of all the glittering cornucopia of Hollywood females, not one had the right stuff to really *become* Scarlett O'Hara.

Their ability to merge totally into the

part would be hampered by the public's memory of them in past roles. Scarlett had to have an indefinable essence all her own, one that she would carry straight from the pages of the book onto the screen. Just what that essence was Selznick couldn't say, except that he'd recognize it when he saw it.

As in a fairy tale, casting directors were sent to all the corners of the country to find Scarlett O'Hara and bring her back to the waiting gates of the studio.

The halls of high schools, colleges, community theaters, and civic auditoriums echoed with the pounding hearts of hopeful stars. The casting searchers—accosted in hotel lobbies and chased through train stations—viewed a total of fourteen hundred girls. And although Alicia Rhett, a Southern belle from Charleston, was discovered and later cast as poor, plain India Wilkes, no Scarlett came to light. Eventually the search was called off, the casting

people returned home, and David Selznick turned his attention to the screenplay.

After much deliberation, he hired Sidney Howard as screenwriter. Howard was not only a movie writer with a string of successes to his name but also a Pulitzer Prize–winning playwright and a farmer with a fair-sized spread in Tyringham, Massachusetts.

He was chosen for his expertise as a *constructionist*, a craftsman capable of stringing a cohesive plot line out of *GWTW*'s sea of characters and subplots.

Sidney Howard took possession of David's copy of the book with the notes scribbled in the margins and fled back to his farm to hammer out the script.

Selznick found Howard's behavior hard to take. He considered himself a tireless contributor to all aspects of his projects, not merely an on-paper producer who sat back in his paneled office and let others do *(Continued on page 24)*

Production designer William Cameron Menzies reviews a few of the 3,000 set sketches produced by the art department. In addition, they designed 200 sets, of which 90 were used.

Art director Lyle Wheeler shows off three of the storyboards used to plot camera angles before shooting. The technique, innovative in its day, was largely copied from the Disney cartoon factory.

David Selznick, Victor Fleming, and cinematographer Ernie Haller ponder a proposed set sketch. Chief electrician James Potevin looks on. The studio caption for this photo pointed out that "Selznick personally supervised each detail in the making of the film."

Because it was built with the entrance off-center, Tara was seldom photographed directly from the front. Florence Yoch, a prominent California landscape architect, designed the as yet unfinished grounds.

Assistant Director Eric Stacey (seated) and Second Assistant Director Ridgeway Callow, coordinating organizational details and checking the complex production schedule mounted on the wall.

A rare side and rear view of Tara under construction.

The first go-round for the movie's opening scene, as Scarlett twists the Tarletons around her little finger. Fred Crane (Brent) is on Scarlett's right, George Bessolo (Stuart) on her left. George changed his surname to Reeves, and in later years soared into America's living rooms as Superman.

Second go-round. The twins now have darker, straighter hair but still no brains when it comes to the likes of Scarlett.

A wardrobe still of the Tarletons to whom, wrote Margaret Mitchell, "raising good cotton, riding well, shooting straight, dancing lightly, squiring the ladies with elegance and carrying one's liquor like a gentleman were the things that mattered."

Scarlett in the famous green-sprigged dress she wears to the Twelve Oaks barbecue.

The Family Circle introduced Vivien Leigh to the reading public in its June 30, 1939, issue, beating out its competition with the first of hundreds of *GWTW*-featured full-color magazine covers.

JUNE 30, 1939   VOL. 14 · NO. 26

THE FAMILY CIRCLE

PRESENTING SCARLETT O'HARA
SEE HARRY EVANS' "HOLLYWOOD DIARY" ON PAGE 10

PRE-PRODUCTION

Gerald (Thomas Mitchell) asks Scarlett if she's been "running about" after Ashley. Note the huge, bulky Technicolor camera being pushed just ahead of them and director George Cukor keeping pace at Gerald's left. Scarlett is still wearing the green-sprigged dress; a later retake will have her gowned in white ruffles.

The sun glints off the snowy shoulders of Vivien Leigh, awaiting a camera setup. Mammy has achieved this unsullied perfection, she has earlier reminded Scarlett, through the liberal application of buttermilk. A track for the camera can be seen at bottom left.

(Continued from page 17)
the work. He expected, even demanded, daily conferences with his writers. Having Howard three thousand miles away was a difficult cross to bear, but he consoled himself by sending the writer a limitless series of script notes and memos.

Three months later Sidney Howard sent back to Selznick the first stage of his work, which he had entitled a "preliminary treatment."

When a writer creates a film script, he generally starts with a *treatment*, a present-tense narrative, rather like a book report, which gives a blow-by-blow outline of the

story. Howard had not done this. He opted instead for a bible, or procedure manual, of how the film would be handled: how to treat sensitive racial issues, i.e., the Ku Klux Klan; which characters would be eliminated (including Scarlett's first child, Wade Hampton Hamilton; her stuffy Charleston and Savannah relatives; and the pre-Tara lives of her parents); and which scenes should be added (some blockade-running incidents with Rhett).

It was a brilliant way to start a difficult project. But Selznick wanted the next phase done on his home turf. Sidney Howard returned to Hollywood, where he spent

Vivien Leigh, clad now in white ruffles for yet another take of Scene One, checks her makeup.

hours locked in script conferences with David and George Cukor, who would be directing the picture.

He then spent six weeks, laboring sixteen hours a day, to get the script finished so he could get back to the memoless quiet of his farm. When it was done, the hefty screenplay ran four hundred pages long and would have used up five and a half hours on the screen. But it was a start. Sidney went home.

Meanwhile Clark Gable's luck was running out. David O. Selznick called him on the phone.

"I knew what was coming," Gable recalled. "I did the sparring and he landed the hard punches," the actor insisting he didn't want to play Rhett.

"That didn't stop David," Gable said. "Being a friend of long standing and knowing him, I knew that it wouldn't. He pointed out that no actor had ever been offered such a chance. There had never been a more talked-of role than Rhett. That was exactly my reason for turning him down."

But to no avail. David struck a deal with MGM. They would loan Gable to Selznick International for the right to distribute the film and fifty percent of the box-office take.

"I could have put up a fight," Gable said. "I didn't. I am glad now that I didn't."

Part of the reason he didn't put up a fight was that he really had no say in the matter. The other reason was that MGM gave him, as a consolation bonus, the funds he needed to divorce his present wife and marry the woman he was wild about, Carole Lombard. In August 1938, he was signed for the part of Rhett Butler.

Scarlett still had not been found. Yet on a bitterly cold night in December 1938, her first scene was scheduled to be filmed. This scene was called the Burning of Atlanta, even though Margaret Mitchell kept pointing out that this was in actuallity only the Confederate's setting fire to their own munitions stores and that the city itself had been burned by the Yankees much later. Scarlett and Rhett were to take a terrifying wagon ride through the conflagration.

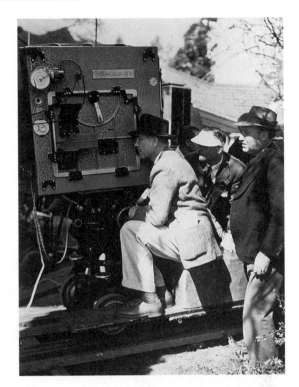

Director Victor Fleming peers past the camera at a setup of Scene One as cinematographer Lee Garmes stands by at his left.

Lyle Wheeler, *GWTW*'s art director, had come up with the idea of actually setting the studio back lot on fire. Forty Acres, as the back lot was called, was a hodgepodge of other sets from other pictures, all standing in rickety profusion like relics from other worlds. These would have to be demolished to make room for the new Atlanta sets still to be built. Wheeler's idea was to kill two birds with one stone—get rid of the old sets by burning them down and simultaneously capturing the fire on film as the burning of Atlanta.

New false fronts were tacked onto the old buildings to give them the veneer of munitions warehouses. The old pagan gate and native village left over from *King Kong* stood ready to play new parts. An elaborate system of oil and water pipes was rigged up behind the buildings to allow control of the flames.

Security guards, studio firemen, city fire departments, cameramen, a horse trainer and extra horses, stunt doubles for Rhett and Scarlett, secretaries, makeup girls, wardrobe ladies, invited guests, Cukor, and Selznick all took their assigned places on the cold, dark lot.

The signal was given, the oil ignited, and a three-hundred-foot wall of flame shot up into the night. Black smoke billowed skyward. The doubles for Rhett and Scarlett raced through the fire.

Selznick's brother, Myron, a noted Hollywood talent agent, appeared at the producer's elbow with a shadowy figure just behind him. "David..."

Selznick, not wanting to be distracted, shrugged him off.

"You're late," he told Myron, eyes on the flames. "The filming's almost over."

"David," Myron persisted, "I want you to meet Scarlett O'Hara."

The shadowy figure stepped forward, green eyes glinting in the half-light. Selznick always maintained that from the moment he first saw Vivien Leigh, the flames of Atlanta playing across her face, he had known she was Scarlett.

(Continued on page 40)

A wardrobe still of Vivien Leigh in the white dress. In the background is Barbara O'Neil (Ellen O'Hara).

David Selznick surprises Vivien with a spur-of-the-moment bouquet from Tara's front lawn.

In this publicity shot, Scarlett, aghast at the news of Ashley's engagement to Melanie, runs off down the driveway, leaving the Tarletons to ask each other, "What do you suppose has gotten into her?"

The studio publicity blurb that went out with this photo read: "…Miss Leigh was selected to play Scarlett O'Hara because she has the dark hair and green eyes of Miss Mitchell's description and because her intelligence, determination and talent foretokened success in the most difficult assignment a Hollywood actress ever faced, the longest sustained part every played on the screen by man or woman… Miss Leigh is shown in more than nine tenths of the 680 master scenes outlined in the script…"

This photograph of a nameless technician and boxes of camera effects, taken just prior to Scarlett's run down the driveway, shows a very different picture of Tara than that seen in the film.

Gerald O'Hara, master of Tara plantation, of whom Miss Mitchell wrote: "There was something vital and earthy and coarse about him..."

Hattie McDaniel (Mammy), Oscar Polk (Pork), and Ben Carter (Jeems) share a quiet momont on the Tara set. All of Carter's scenes, as the Tarletons' ever-present groom, were later deleted.

Gerald's walk with Scarlett was refilmed; Scarlett now wears the demure white ruffles.

A publicity shot of Scarlett and Gerald at Tara.

Vivien Leigh and Victor Fleming (seated, in tie) in a thoughtful moment between takes.

Father and daughter at the beginning of the film's first silhouette shot. "It will come to you, this love of the land," he tells her. "There's no getting away from it if you're Irish."

S.I.P.-108-320

The shot itself— Scarlett and Gerald silhouetted against a flaming sky and Tara's stirring theme.

Ellen returns to Tara after delivering the illegitimate child of Emmy Slattery and Jonas Wilkerson (Victor Jory, at left). "Your child has been born," she says, "and mercifully has died."

A wardrobe still of Oscar Polk in Pork's first costume.

Wardrobe still of Barbara O'Neil in an elegant outfit that is surprisingly unmussed after the trials of midwifery.

George Cukor and Clark Gable on the set of Scarlett's bedroom. Gable's wife, Carole Lombard, was presented with a similar bedspread at the Atlanta movie premiere.

An early makeup and wardrobe still of Hattie McDaniel. Born in Kansas, she had to learn Mammy's Southern Black dialect.

A publicity photo of Vivien Leigh, batting the famous green eyes.

Pork and Mammy arrive at Twelve Oaks in the carriage. This scene never made it into the final film.

CHAPTER THREE

The
FILMING

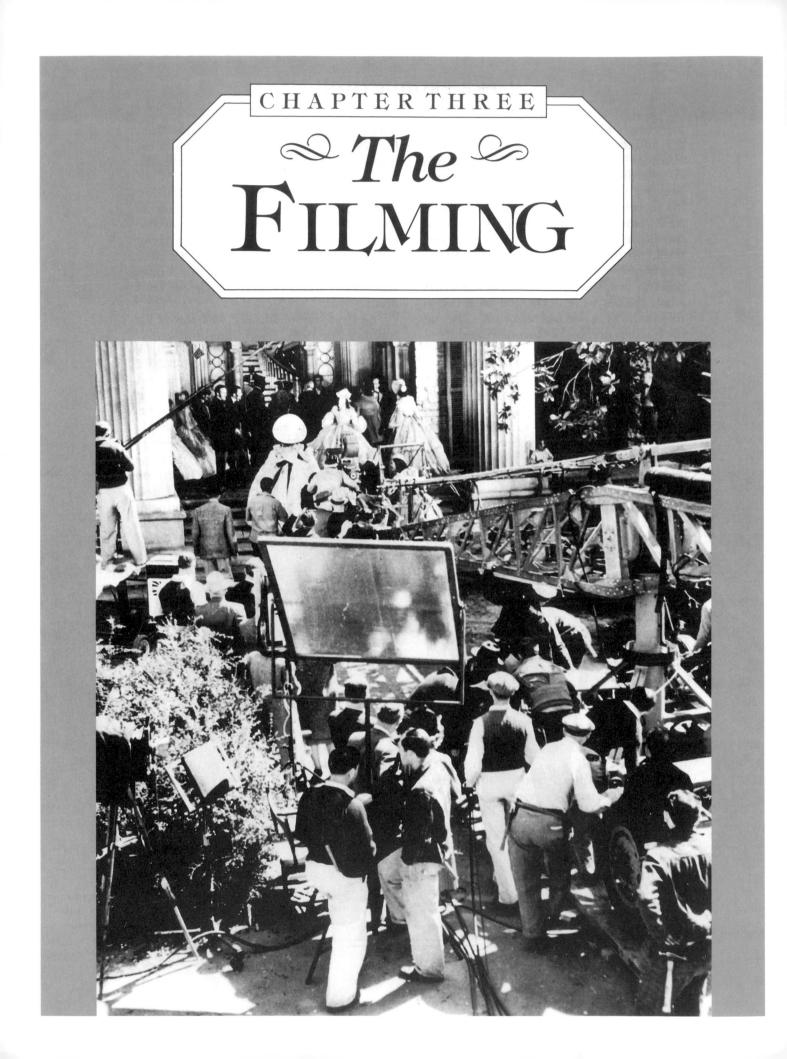

THE FILMING

All during the drama of casting, research, and planning, Selznick had been working on the screenplay. He had used a dozen different writers, from Charles MacArthur (husband of Helen Hayes and coauthor of *The Front Page*) to John Van Druten and Oliver H. P. Garrett to F. Scott Fitzgerald, to "fix" the script. He had them writing on trains, planes, and boats, from Hollywood to New York to Bermuda.

Selznick ultimately applied to Margaret Mitchell. He wrote to her "with what amounts to an almost depressing conviction that you will refuse" for advice. He had his secretary pull apart and cross-index the entire book.

The rewrites were so vast that the resulting mass was dubbed the "rainbow script" for the bevy of different-colored page revisions poking out of it. And still a final version did not exist. But the lack of a script was no hindrance. Filming was about to begin.

Thursday, January 26. In the modest bungalows that lined the streets behind the studio, husbands were leaving for work, children for school, and wives hummed along with the music of Paul Whiteman on the radio as they cleared the breakfast dishes.

On the other side of the chain-link fence, the cast and crew of *GWTW* buzzed with activity. The first day of shooting was under way.

The huge, boxy Technicolor camera was trained on the front porch of Tara. Lee Garmes, the cinematographer, peered past it, along with George Cukor. Vivien Leigh, fetchingly attired in a green sprigged muslin dress, stood ready to flirt with the carrot-haired Tarleton twins.

The "twins," Fred Crane and George Bessolo, were not even related, and since no amount of makeup could make them appear identical, their relationship in the script was amended to the Tarleton "boys." And the camera interpreted their hair as such a vivid orange that it was dark-ened, straightened, and the entire scene reshot several days later. It was reshot yet again, months later, when it was decided that Scarlett would look more virginally sweet sixteen in white ruffles than in the green muslin.

While Scarlett baited the Tarletons on Tara's porch, the screech and thud of saws and hammers rent the air on another part of the back lot.

A world was being created on Forty Acres. All of Atlanta was being built from scratch, including the train station and its massive car barn, the lofty church hospital, Frank's store, Shantytown, the armory where the bazaar was held, Aunt Pittypat's house, and Scarlett's postwar mansion. The set for the city of Atlanta, the largest ever constructed for a single picture, comprised fifty-three buildings and seven thousand feet of streets.

Tara and various rooms within Twelve Oaks, too, were built on the back lot. Only the gardens of the Wilkes plantation and a few scenes of Tara's farther reaches were shot on location.

Trees were planted, sod was laid, huckleberry bushes imported from Oregon to become boxwood hedges. In some cases, trees were built of plaster wrapped around telephone poles. Trucks lumbered in and out of the studio gates, bearing loads of crushed brick to scatter over the sets for the red earth of Georgia.

In the wardrobe department, sewing machines whirred and scissors clattered onto wooden tables. Seamstresses worked feverishly to complete 2,868 costumes, not including 1,230 Confederate uniforms. Three weeks were required just to make one striped dress for Scarlett.

Hats of felt and feathers, silks and lace, were designed and made, along with jewelry, gloves, and handbags. Pantalets of flour sacking shared hanger space with evening gowns in blue net and burgundy velvet.

Wartime costumes (there were twenty-seven versions of Scarlett's calico dress *(Continued on page 54)*

The O'Haras arrive at Twelve Oaks, with the assistance of at least three dozen technicians.

A wardrobe still of Gerald O'Hara in all his finery.

Wardrobe still of Suellen in her barbecue outfit.

Wardrobe still of Howard Hickman as John Wilkes, master of Twelve Oaks and father of Ashley.

A wardrobe still of Alicia Rhett (India Wilkes, Ashley's sister) in the dress she wears as mistress of Twelve Oaks.

Alicia Rhett, an accomplished artist, often sketched other cast members between scenes. Here she captures the likeness of Ann Rutherford as Evelyn Keyes looks on.

The elegant hall and curving staircase of Twelve Oaks.

A wardrobe still of Carroll Nye as Suellen's beau, Frank Kennedy, whom Scarlett scathingly describes as "that old maid in britches."

Wardrobe still of Carreen. Her nickname was a contraction of Caroline Irene.

Wardrobe still of Suellen, properly named Susan Elinor, the 15-year-old sister of Scarlett.

Wardrobe still of Rand Brooks as dewy-eyed Charles Hamilton, Melanie's brother.

The Tarletons, about to abandon their barbecue dates for Scarlett. The blurry figure at bottom left is the Technicolor man with his omnipresent chart.

Clark Gable's first appearance in the film. He is watching Scarlett ascend the stairs in the company of Cathleen Calvert. "Who's that man?" Scarlett asks. "The nasty, dark one."

The studio publicity caption for this photo read: "When the massive Technicolor camera has to follow Vivien Leigh up a winding staircase, it presents some tricky technical problems... The camera is on a movable boom, and the man who operates the giant 'box,' Arthur Arling, assistant cameraman, is seated directly back of the 'blimp,' which houses the camera. Others in the picture are extras and stage technicians."

Scarlett entertains her many beaux.

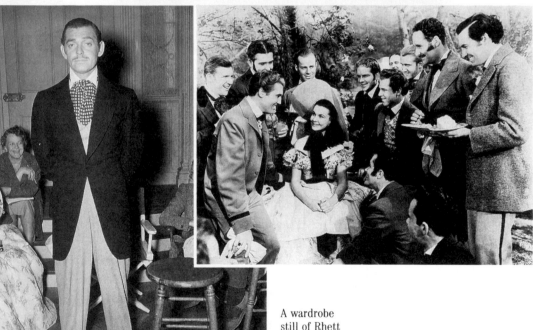

A wardrobe still of Rhett Butler. Behind him, at left, are Vivien Leigh, holding a smoking cigarette, and Susan Myrick.

This scene, entitled "A Young Man Talks to Rhett," although beautifully filmed, was cut from the final production.

Wardrobe still of S. Jackson, a not terribly youthful "Young Man."

S. Jackson and Victor Fleming flank Clark Gable, looking rakish even between takes. The setting is the Twelve Oaks barbecue, filmed at Busch Gardens in Pasadena, California.

Melanie and Ashley in a tête-à-tête at the barbecue.

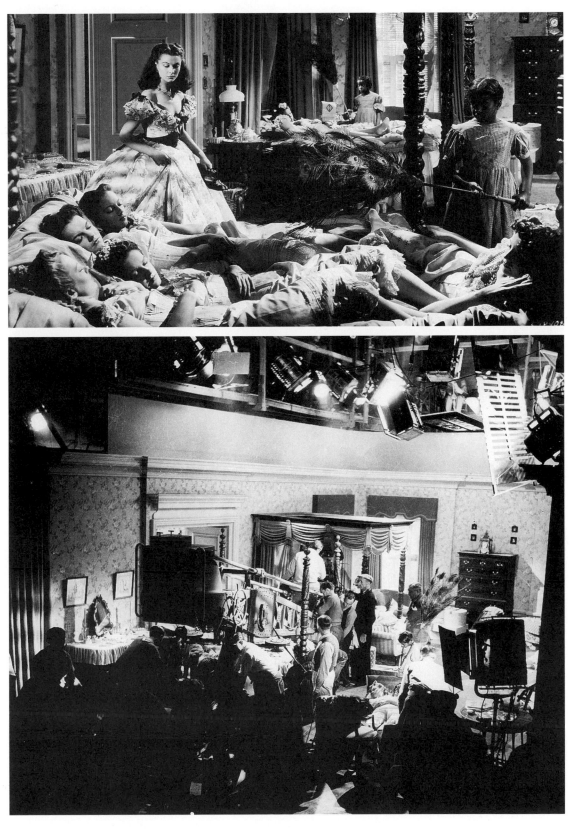

Scarlett sneaks out of the bedroom to confront Ashley with her great love for him. Selznick wanted to show a row of hoopskirted dresses standing alone while their owners slept. Susan Myrick had a difficult time convincing him that this could not be done; if they were rigid enough to stand on their own, it would not be possible to sit in them. He also insisted on keeping the girls' corsets tightened so that busts would not droop. Margaret Mitchell sympathized with Susan, writing: "I wish Mr. Selznick could be put into a corset and laced down to 16 inches and be laid upon a bed with the request that he get some beauty sleep. I think he might then understand the reason for loosened stays."

Filming the "Nap Time" sequence. Notice the bank of hot lights above the set.

(Continued from page 43)

alone) were made and then aged, using a process combining carborundum, sandpaper, emery wheels, fine steel brushes, beeswax, lumber, stone, and dirt.

Property people sought out such diverse items as Bonnie Blue Butler's ornate prancing-horse baby carriage, a historically accurate coffin with trimmings, a cast-iron locomotive bell, contemporary upholstery fabrics, wallpaper, a hobby horse, old-fashioned shovels shaped like the spades on playing cards, and a half dozen flies for a sickroom sequence.

While all this was going on behind the scenes, filming continued in front of the camera.

In quick succession, the events leading up to the barbecue at Twelve Oaks were shot: Gerald's walk with Scarlett across the plantation, Mammy's attempt to convince Scarlett to "eat every mouthful" of breakfast, the O'Hara family at prayer, and Ellen's encounter with dastardly overseer Jonas Wilkerson.

Jonas's scene later had to be reshot with actor Victor Jory when the original Wilkerson, Robert Gleckler, died of uremic poisoning one month into filming.

Susan Myrick, a friend of Margaret Mitchell's who had been hired as an adviser on Southern accents and etiquette, watched every scene. So did Natalie Kalmus, wife of Herb Kalmus, who owned the new Technicolor process and had the right to approve every frame.

The gentlemen talk war in the Twelve Oaks dining room. Gerald is seated at the table; Ashley stands at his left.

Charles Hamilton, with all the naïve desire for war of the county youth, confronts the cynical, sophisticated Captain Butler. In a moment Rhett's views will make him so unpopular that he will, wisely, decide to leave the room.

Gable emerges from his portable dressing room in his barebecue clothes. He was so popular that when he appeared sans undershirt in *It Happened One Night*, sales of that particular item dipped to almost nothing.

Cukor consulted with the ladies after each take. "Okay for Dixie?" If Susan nodded in agreement, the scene was considered final; if she felt the accents weren't right, it was redone with her mild coaching.

Natalie Kalmus, on the other hand, was inclined to be dictatorial, frequently insisting that an entire scene be reshot because some color or another looked wrong on film. Even after an item of clothing or upholstery had already been made and used in a scene, Mrs. Kalmus might order it changed. And her word had to be obeyed.

More shooting script somehow appeared day by day, like magic. Girls in silks and ribbons and lace whirled across the floor in the bazaar sequence, carefully choreographed by Frank Floyd and Eddie Prinz. Rhett brought Scarlett a hat from gay Paris. Melanie gave birth to baby Beau, assisted in her labor pains by Cukor twisting her ankle under the bedclothes whenever he wanted a contraction. Rhett arrived with his stolen horse and wagon to rescue the women and child from the approaching Yankees.

Then, in the midst of all this, George Cukor left the production. The reason teetered somewhere between Selznick firing

Twelve Oaks's magnificent parquet-floored hall. The nearer door leads into the library.

Vivien Leigh and Leslie Howard having much more fun in the library than Scarlett and Ashley do.

him and Cukor quitting in a huff, but the general consensus was the tried-and-true "creative differences." Cukor felt that, as the director, he should have the greatest control—over script, style, and substance—while Selznick was determined to guide him along every step of the way. Friction between the two escalated daily, coming to a head on February 13, when Cukor refused to go any further under the present regime.

Selznick had to find another director. Checking around at MGM, he pulled Victor Fleming off the set of *The Wizard of Oz*, where three weeks remained until the completion of filming, and set him to reading *Gone With the Wind*.

Fleming was appalled at the amorphous mass of pages set before him. He told Selznick in language that would do a longshoreman proud that his script was no good, and refused to begin shooting until a final screenplay had been drafted.

By this time, Selznick was in a panic. With a cast and crew idling to the tune of $50,000 a day, he *had* to get a script written—and fast.

Ben Hecht was the man chosen for the job. Hecht, a veteran screenwriter (and coauthor of *The Front Page* with Charles MacArthur, who had already put in time on the project), agreed to take on the task for a generous hazard pay of $10,000 for two week's work. And it turned out to be a battle-wearying job, indeed.

Sunday morning. Selznick, Fleming, and Hecht, fortified with coffee, arrived at the studio offices. Hecht had never read the book, and although the other two told him the whole story, he claimed he never did understand it. It was too long and had entirely too many characters. After an hour of searching, the original Sidney Howard script—being the only one with a coherent plot line—was unearthed and used as a guide.

But Hecht never read that version, either. Instead Selznick and Fleming acted out the entire story, scene by scene, burly David playing the parts of Scarlett and Ashley, and Fleming doing Rhett and Melanie. Hecht sat on the sofa, banging out the words on a typewriter as they went along.

This went on for five endless days and nights, at the close of which a blood vessel dramatically, and rather gorily, burst in Fleming's right eye and Selznick collapsed on the sofa in a sleep so deep, the other two feared it was a coma.

Hecht stayed on for another week, cleaning up various points, then prepared to leave for New York. David begged him to stay another two weeks, for another $10,000. Hecht refused, saying there wasn't enough money in the world for that kind of slave labor.

But the script was finished. Filming could resume.

Shooting had not progressed entirely in sequence because some of the sets had not been completed, but by this time Twelve Oaks was ready to go, and the indoor events of the barbecue were filmed, including the county girls gossiping on the staircase and napping upstairs, and Scarlett's confession of love to Ashley.

The outdoor scenes were shot later, on location at Busch Gardens, an estate built on money from the brewery trade, in Pasadena, California.

Now Selznick decided to replace Lee Garmes as cinematographer because of differences in the look of the finished product. Garmes wanted, and was working toward, softer shades of colors, while David had in mind the richer, more vivid tones the picture ended up with. The two parted amicably enough, and Ernest Haller took over, completing the Twelve Oaks library scene that Garmes had started.

While the change from Garmes to Haller was painless, Cukor's replacement with Fleming was the source of endless friction among the ladies of the cast.

Gable was delighted. He and Fleming were great buddies from way back, having shared work (Fleming directed Gable in *Test Pilot*, among other films) and play.

(Continued on page 187)

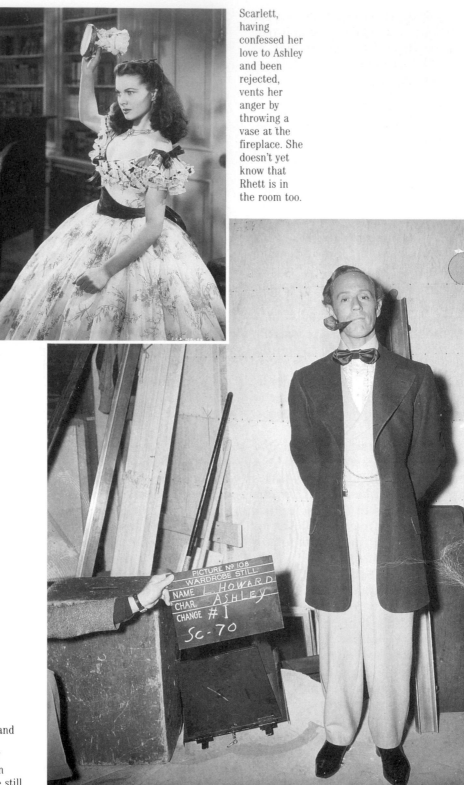

Scarlett, having confessed her love to Ashley and been rejected, vents her anger by throwing a vase at the fireplace. She doesn't yet know that Rhett is in the room too.

PICTURE Nº 108
WARDROBE STILL
NAME L. HOWARD
CHAR. ASHLEY
CHANGE #1
Sc-70

Leslie Howard and various pieces of lumber in wardrobe still number one for Ashley.

Victor Fleming, Leslie Howard, and Vivien Leigh consult "the Book."

Marjorie Reynolds (the blonde on the top left), Evelyn Keyes, and Alicia Rhett gossip about Scarlett, unaware she is standing just beside the staircase. Melanie, of course, doesn't believe a word of it. "She's just high-spirited," she says placatingly.

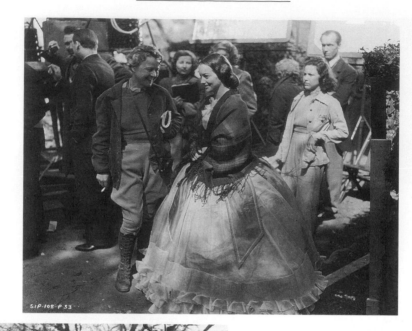

A tearful farewell as Ashley leaves Melanie to join the Confederate Army. The groom holding Rebel's bridle doesn't appear in the film; neither does the brave studio man on the ground, grasping a hoof.

Susan Myrick and Olivia de Havilland in front of Twelve Oaks. Miss Myrick, a writer for the *Macon* (Georgia) *Telegraph* and the daughter of a Confederate soldier, was recommended to the studio by Margaret Mitchell because of "her common sense and utter lack of sentimentality about what is tearfully known as 'The Old South.'"

Leslie Howard astride Rebel, the famous show horse, sporting an authentically cropped tail. This scene was filmed at Busch Gardens in March 1939.

The family gathers for Scarlett's wedding to Charles Hamilton, but the new bride has eyes only for Ashley.

Tara's lovely parlor, decorated with flowers for the wedding.

Scarlett in her bridal gown. The dress was actually her mother's, and Walter Plunkett was proud of the fact that he had purposely made it too big—the wedding was so rushed that there wasn't time to take it in.

Wardrobe stills for Scarlett's wedding to Charles:

Wardrobe still of Oscar Polk in costume number two.

Ellen. Miss O'Neil's name was misspelled on the wardrobe board here, and also in the film credits.

The Tarletons in their dashing uniforms.

The dapper Mr. Plunkett passes last-minute approval on the dress Melanie wears to Scarlett's wedding.

The groom. The sword at his side will figure prominently in a later scene.

Brother and sister share a happy moment at the wedding. India was probably pleased to have Scarlett out of circulation, but in the final film she isn't at the ceremonies.

Wardrobe still of Mammy in mourning clothes.

Wardrobe still of Scarlett in the mourning dress necessitated by Charles's death from measles.

Wardrobe still of Mammy, wearing a lace collar for Scarlett's wedding.

Ellen comforts her daughter after the death of Charles, but Scarlett is mourning more for the parties she cannot attend than for her lost husband.

Wardrobe still of Ellen in mourning dress. Miss O'Neil's name is still misspelled.

John Frederics was, as the studio publicity department advised, "America's most outstanding designer of feminine headgear, shown holding two of the creations Scarlett… will wear in the film." Good PR, although none of his hats ended up in the finished movie.

An extremely rare photo of Vivien Leigh modeling one of Mr. Frederics' creations.

Another rare shot of Vivien in a Frederics hat.

A set still of the Atlanta bazaar, festively draped with sashes, bunting, flags, and streamers. The board names George Cukor as director, but most of this sequence was later reshot by Victor Fleming.

The dashing Captain Butler enters the bazaar. His cape, top hat, and gloves, while the height of elegance, are not seen in the final film.

Rhett engages Scarlett in conversation. Margaret Mitchell, after viewing stills of "Scarlett's widow's bonnet and long veil in the midst of the decollete gowns of the Atlanta belles," wrote to a friend, "I cannot imagine even Scarlett having such bad taste as to wear a hat at an evening party."

George Cukor instructs Gable and Leigh in the finer points of bazaar behavior.

Melanie sacrifices her wedding ring for the good of the Cause. The one-armed basket carrier is Ned Davenport, in real life the son of Harry Davenport (Dr. Meade).

Grande dame of Atlanta society, Mrs. Merriwether (Jane Darwell, in black)—oversees her daughter, Maybelle (Mary Anderson) and Colonel Tim Longeran. Behind her is Mrs. Elsing (Mary Young) and a whole platform full of nosy town biddies. This scene, and the character of Mrs. Elsing, were eliminated from the final film.

Dr. Meade makes a startling announcement—to raise money for the hospital, gentlemen will have to bid for dances with the ladies.

A wardrobe still of Harry Davenport (Dr. Meade), a fine actor who first trod the boards in 1871 at the age of 5.

Maybelle Merriwether arm in arm with Rene Picard (Albert Morin). In the book they were eventually married; the movie did not comment.

Wardrobe still of Albert Morin as Rene Picard. His costume is the uniform of the Zouave, a New Orleans military unit.

Mrs. Merriwether comforts Melanie as Mrs. Elsin and Aunt Pittypat (Laura Hope Crews) look on. This scene, along with Mrs. Elsing's others, was later cut from the picture.

Wardrobe still of Aunt Pittypat. As Charles describes her in the book: "She is the most helpless soul—just like a sweet, grown-up child..."

Wardrobe stills for the bazaar:

Jane Darwell as the Mrs. Merriwether.

Leona Roberts as Mrs. Meade, the doctor's wife.

Mary Young as Mrs. Elsing.

Filming the dance sequence at the bazaar. George Cukor, seated on the camera truck, is delighted with the action.

Walter Plunkett's original sketch for the mourning costume Scarlett wears to the bazaar. The wardrobe department produced 450 costume sketches, of which 377 were made by Plunkett.

Gable approaches the camera with determination during a break in filming. Vivien Leigh can be seen in the background.

George Cukor gives a bit of direction that brings smiles from his principals.

Rhett, having shocked the crowd by bidding for the Widow Hamilton, and Scarlett, having shocked them more by accepting, lead the Virginia Reel. The studio caption for this photo read: "Gable surprised everyone with his ability as a dancer, although he had some difficulty getting rid of the tap routines left over from his last venture as a dancer in *Idiot's Delight*." Said Gable of Miss Leigh: "She dances beautifully."

The Technicolor technician (center) dashes away with his chart before the action starts for the Virginia Reel.

Something amusing lights up the faces of Clark Gable and Vivien Leigh.

Cukor and Plunkett in deep discussion on set the set of the bazaar.

A wardrobe still of Gable in his bazaar finery.

Cukor, Gable, and an unknown member of the bazaar orhestra.

Gable takes on Leigh at a game of Chinese checkers between takes.

Rhett has brought Scarlett a hat from Paris. "It's my duty to our brave boys at the front to keep our girls at home looking pretty."

Wardrobe still of Gable in outfit number three.

Filming the Paris Hat sequence. Cukor leans on the camera at top center; Lee Garmes stands besides the draperies.

Selznick and Fleming confer on the set of Aunt Pittypat's Parlor.

Aunt Pittypat's parlor charmingly reflects her fussy, frivolous nature, from the owl lamp behind the settee to the flower-laden figurines on the mantel.

The entire scene was refilmed. Scarlett now has a new hairstyle, and Rhett wears a different shirt and tie.

"Ashley's safe!" Scarlett and Melanie absorb this news from the casualty lists, while Uncle Peter (Eddie Anderson) stands by the carriage. Uncle Peter, ostensibly Aunt Pitty's coachman, who has raised the orphaned Melanie and Charles from early childhood, makes all the decisions for scatter-brained Pitty, and is in reality the head of the household.

Melanie and the Meades, whose son, Darcy, has been killed at Gettysburg. Their younger boy, Phil (Jackie Moran), wants to enlist and make the Yankees sorry. "Do you think it would help your mother to have you off getting shot too?" Melanie counsels.

Peachtree Street circa 1862. In the foreground Gable and Leigh rehearse a scene. Notice the wealth of period detail in the costumes, carriages, and set. Eddie Anderson, seated on the coachman's box, was well known on radio (and later television) as Jack Benny's long-suffering manservant, Rochester.

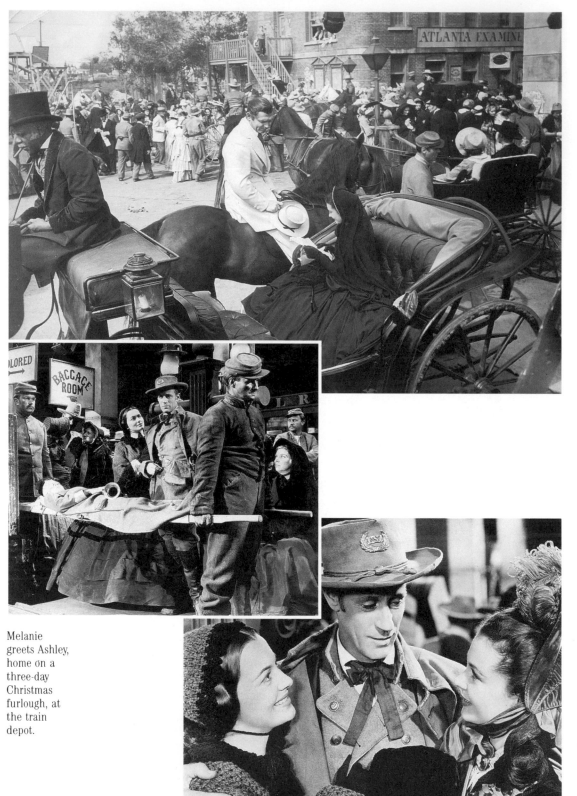

Melanie greets Ashley, home on a three-day Christmas furlough, at the train depot.

Scarlett, wearing the Paris bonnet from Rhett, also welcomes him home.

Ashley in his dashing cavalry officer's uniform.

A publicity portrait of Melanie in the costume she wears to meet Ashley at the depot.

Christmas dinner at Aunt Pittypat's. "Why did you say there wasn't enough [Madeira]?" Pitty asks Uncle Peter, going on to explain the genealogy of every family member who had anything to do with the wine. "But we mustn't drink it all at once because it *is* the last."

Wardrobe still of Uncle Peter in the costume he wears to chase the "last chicken in Atlanta" for the family's Christmas dinner. This delightful scene, in which rain-soaked Peter coaxes the fowl ("We's et all your wives; we's et all your little chicks. You got nobody to worry your head about leavin'") was directed by William Cameron Menzies, here standing in the background.

Melanie and Ashley ascend the stairs to the bedroom.

As Ashley prepares to leave again for the battlefront, Scarlett once more confesses her love, but he only makes her promise to take care of Melanie.

Scarlett watches Melanie walk away to an intimacy with Ashley that she cannot attain. Despite her unladylike thoughts, Scarlett looks, in this photo, strikingly like her very ladylike mother.

A stunning
publicity
portrait of
Vivien Leigh
as Scarlett.

Scarlett and Melanie nurse a Reminiscent Soldier (Cliff Edwards, the voice of Jiminy Cricket) in the church hospital. The shadows on the wall are not facing the same way as the ladies, but nonetheless it is a beautiful scene.

Belle Watling (Ona Munson), the town madam, offers the ladies money for the Cause; Melanie is the only one kind, and perhaps, brave enough to take it.

The horrors of the hospital inflict themselves on Scarlett.

Unable to take any more, she flees from the hospital into the havoc of the evacuating citizenry. This scene was dangerous to shoot; notice the terror on the face of the horse.

A tired-looking Vivien Leigh rests between takes during the evacuation sequence.

Scarlett dashes across Peachtree Street. Note the camera tracks in the dirt.

Scarlett encounters Big Sam (Everett Brown) and other field workers from Tara, en route to shore up Atlanta's battlements. Though she doesn't look it here, she is delighted to see them.

"A star on his day off," the original studio caption read. Gable visits with Vivien and Victor on the set. The wardrobe department's attention to detail is evident in the tear in the bodice of her dress.

A wardrobe
still of Gable.

Rhett rescues
Scarlett from
the onrushing
crowd.

Scarlett extends her search for the doctor to the interior of the train shed.

Fleming rides high above the crowd on the camera platform as it passes over the railway yard and the Confederate flag.

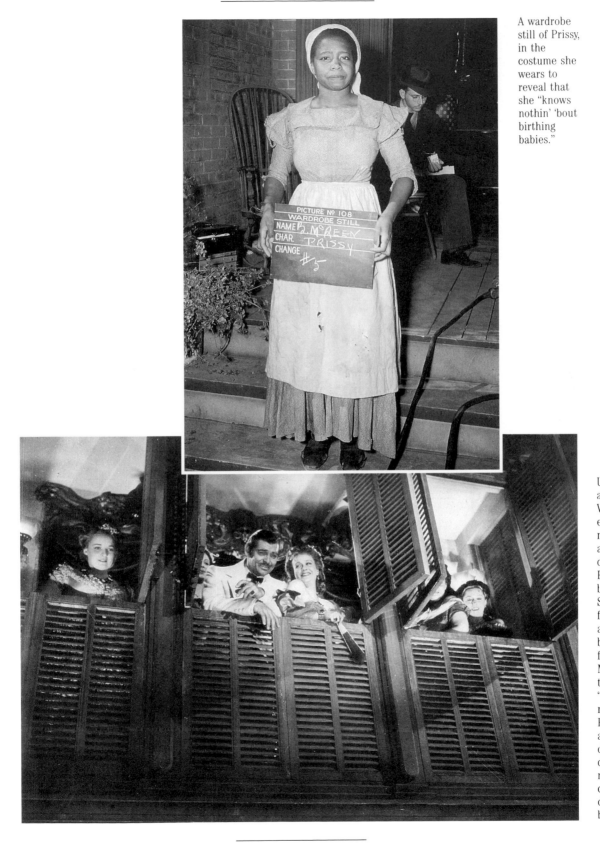

A wardrobe still of Prissy, in the costume she wears to reveal that she "knows nothin' 'bout birthing babies."

Upstairs at Belle Watling's establishment. They're all looking down at Prissy, who's been sent by Scarlett to find Rhett and have him bring a wagon for her, Melanie, and the new baby. "Well, it was mostly me," Prissy boasts about the delivery. "I don't expect no doctor could have done no better."

Rhett and Scarlett in the wagon as they weave through crowds of weary soldiers leaving Atlanta.

George Cukor and David Selznick on the night the fire scene was filmed, probably prior to the appearance of Vivien Leigh.

Out of town at last, on the road to Tara. Doubles fill in for Prissy, Scarlett, and Rhett as the crew prepares the scene.

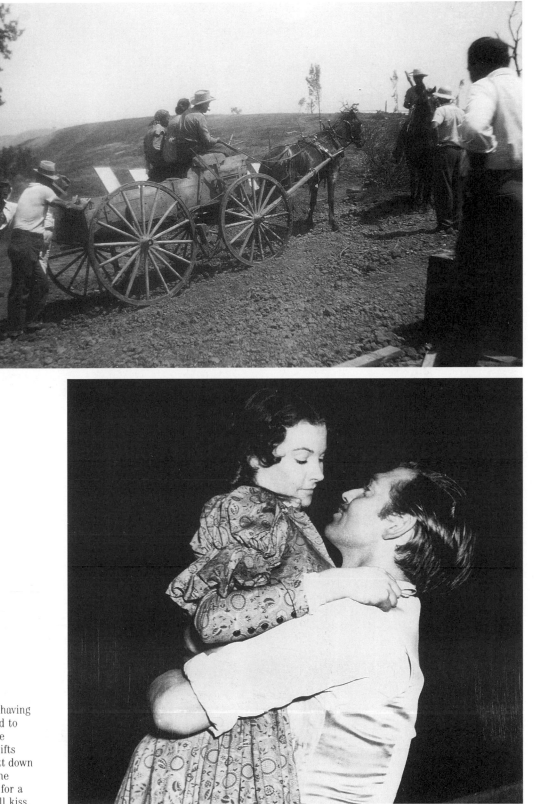

Rhett, having decided to join the Army, lifts Scarlett down from the wagon for a farewell kiss.

THE FILMING

The crew prepares for the shot where Scarlett hides under the bridge, in a driving rain, with the wagon. Although it looks sunny here, the weather obliged with a real rainstorm.

Facing page. "I love you more than I've ever loved any woman," he says.

Twelve Oaks has been destroyed by the Yankees; in this production photo Melanie and Scarlett stare at its ruined shell and at the grave of Ashley's father. In the film, however, editing has made it appear that Scarlett is in what's left of the house.

Bone-weary and numbed by the horror of what she's seen, Scarlett arrives at Tara; her only thought is to be comforted by her mother.

Gerald embraces Scarlett; she doesn't notice the vacant look in his eyes.

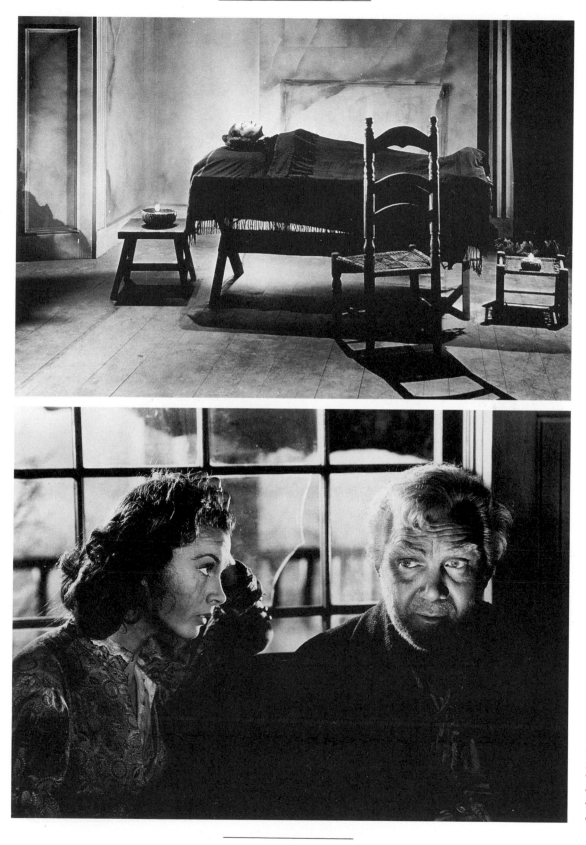

The awful truth—Ellen is dead, of typhoid contracted while nursing Emmy Slattery. Notice the wicks burning in gourds filled with oil; all the candles are gone.

Scarlett asks Gerald how they will manage "We must ask your mother," he answers. "Mrs. O'Hara will know what's to be done."

Home, but more alone than ever. Her mother is dead, her father out of his mind with grief, her sisters ill, and the servants waiting anxiously for her guidance.

The field hands have gone. There is no one left at Tara to pick cotton but the family and the house servants. The cotton seen here is the drugstore variety, glued on to stalks by the set department.

A rare photo of Prissy picking cotton.

The crew sets up for the cotton-picking sequence. Victor Fleming stands to the left of the camera, Evelyn Keyes and Vivien Leigh to the right. The scene was filmed in Calabasas, California, a region of rolling hills about 50 miles north of the studio.

Sue Myrick and Ann Rutherford consult the script on location in Calabasas.

Suellen says she hates Tara and receives a sound slap from Scarlett for sharing her opinion.

Evelyn Keyes and Ann Rutherford drinking imaginary water from the well on the Tara set.

Ann and Evelyn share a smile with their director. Harry Evans wrote of Fleming in a June 1939 issue of *The Family Circle*: "He calls all the girls 'Darling' and treats them as if they were his kids."

Pork, Scarlett, and Mammy near the cotton patch. Prissy is in the background.

Vivien Leigh studies her script on the set.

A Yankee Deserter (Paul Hurst) accosts Scarlett on the stairs. He doesn't know she is hiding a pistol behind the folds of her dress.

After shooting the deserter, Scarlett tries to drag his body out of the house, but his blood is smearing the floorboards. "Give me your nightgown, Melly; I'll wad it round his head," she says.

Gerald announces great news—the war is over.

Jonas Wilkerson and his carpetbagger companion (Ernest Whitman) ride in comfort while the returning veterans struggle along on foot.

Mammy makes Frank Kennedy give her his lice-ridden clothes for boiling. "Now scrub yourself with that strong lye soap," she tells him, " 'Fore I come in there and do it myself."

Suellen thinks Mammy is treating Frank badly. "You'd be a sight more humiliated if Mr. Kennedy's lice gets on you," Mammy retorts.

Melanie chats with a hungry soldier (Philip Trent), one of many who have stopped at Tara for food on the long road home. Prissy and Pork are serving food in the background.

Frank Kennedy finally asks for permission to marry Suellen. Scarlett grants it; "at least it'll be one less mouth to feed," she says later.

Mammy, Melanie, and Scarlett watch as another weary soldier turns up the drive to Tara. And now Melanie realizes that it is Ashley!

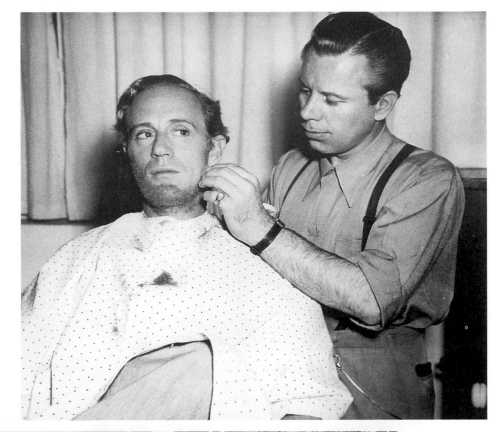

Makeup artist Monty Westmore applies the beard stubble he created for Leslie Howard in the sequence, Ashley's Return from the War. Westmore, head of the makeup department, faced such challenges as making up 1,230 extras in a single day. Fortunately he had 34 assistants.

Pork tells Scarlett, over a vat of boiling soap, that $300 in additional taxes have been levied on Tara.

Scarlett goes to Ashley for advice about the tax money. But Ashley has neither money nor advice. He's mostly interested in, as he puts it, "talking tommyrot about civilization."

Scarlett and Ashley in the paddock. Ashley admits he loves her but he is bound by honor to Melanie.

A publicity
shot of
Scarlett and
Ashley in the
Paddock
Scene.

Wardrobe
still of Ashley
in his
Paddock
Scene garb.

Emmy Slatter (Isabel Jewel) and oily Jonas Wilkerson offer to buy Tara from Scarlett.

Wardrobe still of Isabel Jewel as Emmy Slattery.

Gerald, incensed by Wilkerson's overture, unties the Yankee cavalryman's horse as Pork stands by.

These portraits of Scarlett and Rhett were painted for the 1967 release. Note that Scarlett's neckline has been lowered considerably, an artistic license of which Mammy would never approve.

Gerald and Scarlett on the grounds of Tara, more alike than they realize.

The men at
the barbecue
hover around
Scarlett.

Scarlett
beckons Ash-
ley into the
library at
Twelve Oaks.

Melanie and Ashley on the terrace at Twelve Oaks. "I'll love you just as I do now until I die," she tells him.

Scarlett and Gerald at sunset, surrounded by the beauty of Tara.

Melanie and baby Beau look after a returning Confederate soldier on the steps of Tara.

Melanie hesitates at removing her nightgown so they can wrap the dead Yankee's bloody head in it. "Oh, don't be silly," Scarlett says. "I won't look at you."

Scarlett and Rhett in the wagon as they flee Atlanta.

On the road to Tara, Rhett pulls Scarlett to him in a passionate embrace.

A close shot of Scarlett laboring in the cotton fields after the war.

The Paris hat sequence: Rhett and Scarlett parry over whether he'll kiss her or not.

The newly-wed couple at Tara after the honeymoon.

She's happy again—Rhett has said she can have Tara *and* a house in town.

Scarlett in the dress she wears to Ashley's birthday party.

Scarlett admires her newly purchased finery in a New Orleans shop.

Scarlett and Rhett feature prominently on original lobby posters from the 1939 premiere in Atlanta.

A 1941 advertising poster. Note the slogan, "Nothing cut but the price!"

Inserts displayed by neighborhood theaters. The one on the left dates from 1939, the one on the right is for the 1941 release.

An early poster from 1939.

Another early poster. Note that MGM has begun billing GWTW as "The Greatest Motion Picture Ever Made."

An original 1939 poster, updated for the 1941 general release by the addition of the "Limited Engagement" phrasing below by the artwork. The embrace pictured is from the honeymoon sequence.

A GWTW paint book produced by the Merrill Publishing Company in 1940.

An advertising poster circa 1947.

A theater poster, called a *one-sheet*, from 1941.

The cardboard cover of the press book sent to theater owners by MGM.

The artwork for this one-sheet was created in 1967 when the film was released for 70-mm showings.

A window card used to advertise the film in 1941.

A 1947 poster, with Rhett and Scarlett as passionate as ever.

Gerald on horseback, chasing after Jonas and Emmy.

Carreen and Suellen watch in horror as Gerald, attempting to jump the fence, is thrown from the horse.

Gerald has been killed in the fall from the horse. Scarlett gives his gold pocket watch to Pork. In the novel, Pork has risked his life and saved the family from starvation more than once by roaming the countryside, "liberating" foodstuffs.

Over Mammy's objections, Scarlett takes down "Miz Ellen's portieres" to make into a new dress; she wants to impress Rhett so he'll give her the tax money to save Tara. Notice the rags stuffed in the broken windowpanes.

Jailed in
Atlanta,
Rhett plays
poker with
his Yankee
captors:
The Yankee
Captain
(Robert
Elliott); his
Poker Playing
Captains
(George
Meeker and
Willis Clark);
and the
Corporal
(Irving
Bacon),
standing. The
movie never
makes it
clear why
Rhett is being
held; in the
novel, it was
on a charge
of murder.

Rhett greets
Scarlett in
his cell in the
"horse jail"
while the
corporal
looks on.

Rhett is delighted to see Scarlett again, and pleased that she's not dressed in rags. She tells him everything's going well at Tara.

Gable and Leigh, in contrasting attitudes, resting on the jail set.

Walter Plunkett shows off his original sketch of Scarlett's drapery dress

Another view of the costume sketch. In both book and film, this entire outfit was made in a single evening.

The corporal helps Belle from her carriage as she arrives to visit Rhett in jail.

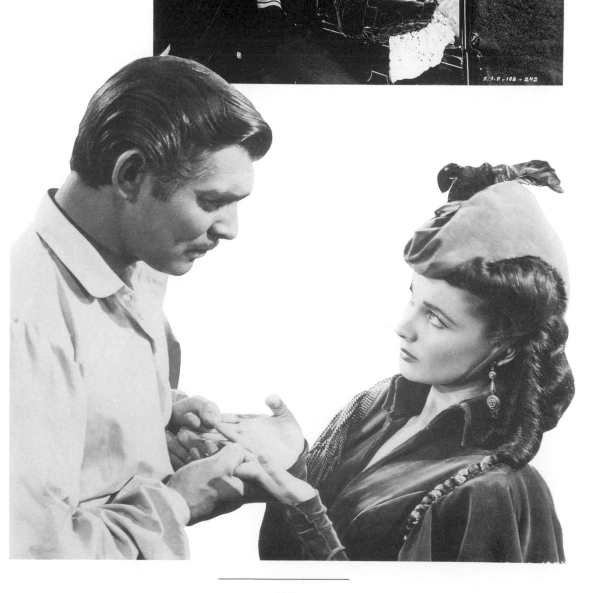

Scarlett's hands turn her words to lies. "You've been working like a field hand," Rhett tells her. Angered because she has come to see him only for her own gain, he sends her packing.

"It must be funny," says the studio caption for this photo of Susan Myrick, Ona Munson, and Walter Plunkett.

Scarlett and Mammy thread their way down Peachtree Street through the hustle of carpetbaggers and freedmen.

Suddenly Frank Kennedy appears in front of his prosperous new store.

Scarlett holds her green velvet skirts above the mud of Peachtree Street.

Frank drives Mammy and Scarlett to Aunt Pittypat's house. The looks on his and Mammy's faces are because Scarlett has just told him, untruthfully, that Suellen is marrying someone else.

Back at Tara, Scarlett tells Melanie and Ashley that she has married Frank, and that she wants Ashley to help her start a lumber mill. Ashley doesn't want to; he's been planning to go into banking up North. "Why, how unchivalrous," Melanie chides him.

Scarlett has bought a lumber mill outside of town. Here she talks to Johnny Gallegher (J. M. Kerrigan), the foreman, about the convict laborers. Ashley and Frank are standing behind her.

Ashley, Frank, and Scarlett at the mill.

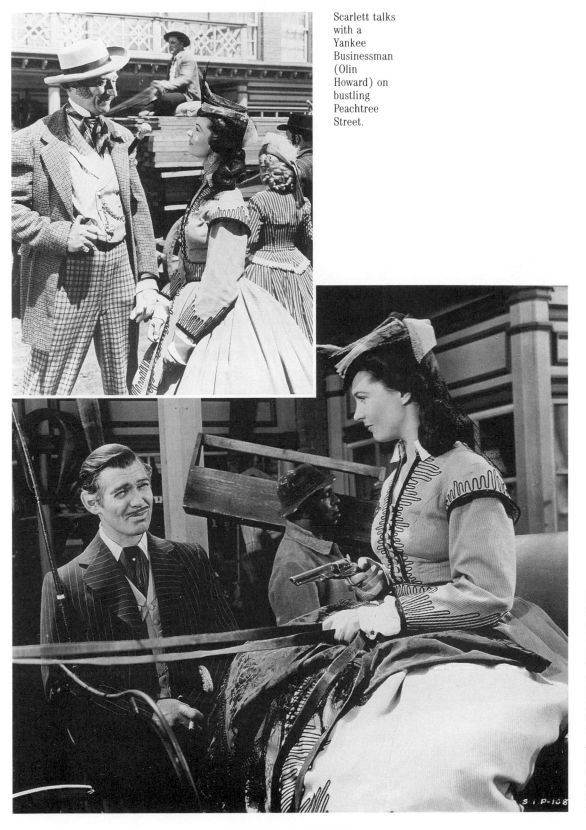

Scarlett talks with a Yankee Businessman (Olin Howard) on bustling Peachtree Street.

Rhett and Scarlett outside of Frank's store. She's on her way to the mill; to get to it she must pass through dangerous Shantytown. About the pistol she says, "I can shoot straight if I don't have to shoot far."

Victor
Fleming
instructs
Vivien Leigh
on driving
away in the
carriage.

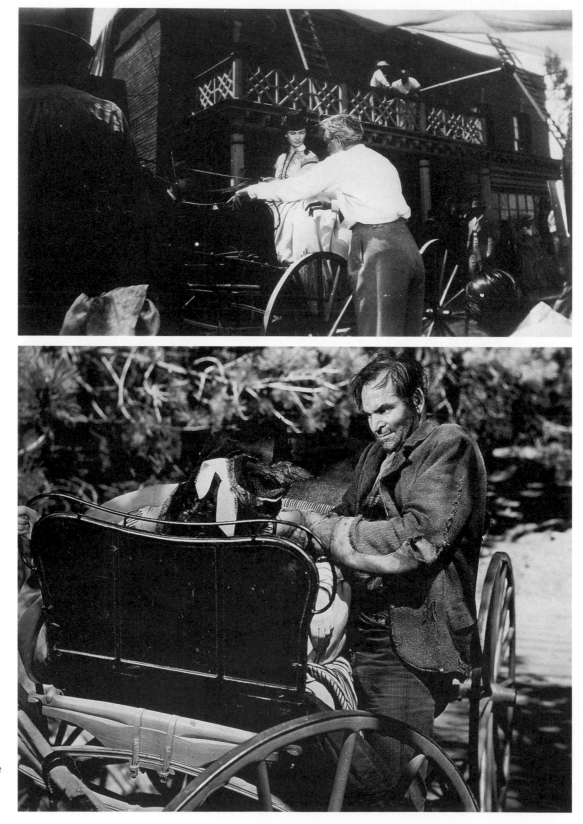

Scarlett is
attacked
on the
Shantytown
bridge by a
Renegade
(Yakima
Canutt).
Canutt, a
respected
stuntman,
was Gable's
double in the
Burning of
Atlanta
sequence.

Big Sam
rescues
Scarlett.

Frank tells
Big Sam to go
back to Tara
where it's
safe. Notice
the gun in
Frank's hand.

Rhett comes
looking for
Ashley and
the others.
India advises
Melanie not
to tell him
where they
are.

A wardrobe
still of Carroll
Nye as Frank
Kennedy. He
was the
makeup
department's
most difficult
case; much
younger than
the character
he portrayed,
he had to be
carefully
aged.

The ladies
have a sewing
circle in
Melanie's
parlor. Their
men are
out at
Shantytown,
"cleaning out
the woods"
after the
attack on
Scarlett.
Scarlett,
however, is
the only one
who doesn't
know what's
going on.

Tom, a Yankee Captain (Ward Bond), and his soldiers are also looking for Ashley. Bond was apparently comfortable on a horse; in later years he starred as the leader of television's *Wagon Train.*

Rhett and Ashley meet Tom in the doorway. He doesn't want to let them through, but Melanie persists even though it's clear they've been drinking. What's not clear is that Ashley's been shot; that's why he's clutching his coat.

Rhett tells Melanie and the Captain that they've been at Belle Watling's establishment while Melly bristles with righteous indignation. Said Olivia de Havilland of this scene: "Melly quite suddenly displays a fine courage and control completely lacking in Scarlett for the moment. With Ashley so badly hurt, it is the soft-spoken, gentle Melanie who takes charge—she was the one person who functioned, and her self-control, intelligence, and poise, yes, and surprising ingenuity—saved her husband, Rhett Butler, and Dr. Meade from great disaster. I think this scene, as much as any other, shows the important facts of Melanie's character—the facts so often hidden."

With the Yankees gone, Dr. Meade attends to Ashley's wound. Notice, however, that this photo has caught Mammy seated on the hat rack, talking to one of the soldiers.

Belle makes a nighttime visit to Melanie. She has heard that Melly is planning to call on her but "it wouldn't be fittin'," she says. Melanie thanks her for saving Ashley. Belle takes it in stride. "And, Miz Wilkes, if you see me on the street you don't have to speak to me. I'll understand."

Frank Kennedy has been killed during the raid on Shantytown. Rhett now comes calling on Scarlett at Aunt Pittypat's house. Scarlett, tipsy on brandy, bursts into tears. She's not crying for Frank but because she's afraid she'll go to hell for stealing him from Suellen.

Rhett proposes marriage to Scarlett. "I am fond of you," she says. "If I said I was madly in love with you, you'd know I was lying." But she accepts his offer.

Fleming, Gable, and Leigh prepare to film the Riverboat Cabin scene from the Butlers' honeymoon. A technician uses a light meter in the foreground.

The cancan dancers in all their petticoated glory.

Scarlett and Rhett dine at a New Orleans restaurant on their honeymoon. Notice the lovebirds on her dress, the cancan dancers in the background.

While in New Orleans, Scarlett goes on a shopping spree. She buys nothing for Mammy because the lady doesn't approve of her new marriage; Rhett buys her a red silk petticoat because he admires her honesty.

Facing page. Rhett and Scarlett return to Tara after their honeymoon. This is where he tells her the words she'll later remember: "You get your strength from the red earth of Tara." But right now she's happy because he's told her she can return the plantation to its old glory *and* have a fine house in Atlanta.

Scarlett and Rhett embrace after her nightmare in their New Orleans hotel room. This shot was the basis for an early *GWTW* poster.

A wardrobe still of Scarlett in her hotel scene nightgown.

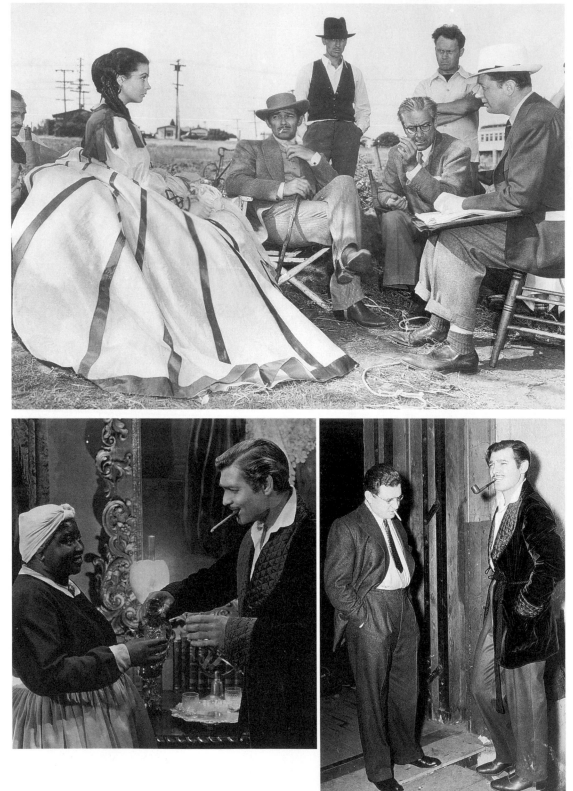

Vivien Leigh, Clark Gable, Victor Fleming, and Reggie Callow seated on the Tara set.

Scarlett has just given birth to a baby girl; Rhett pours Mammy a drink in celebration.

Selznick and Gable in a thoughtful moment.

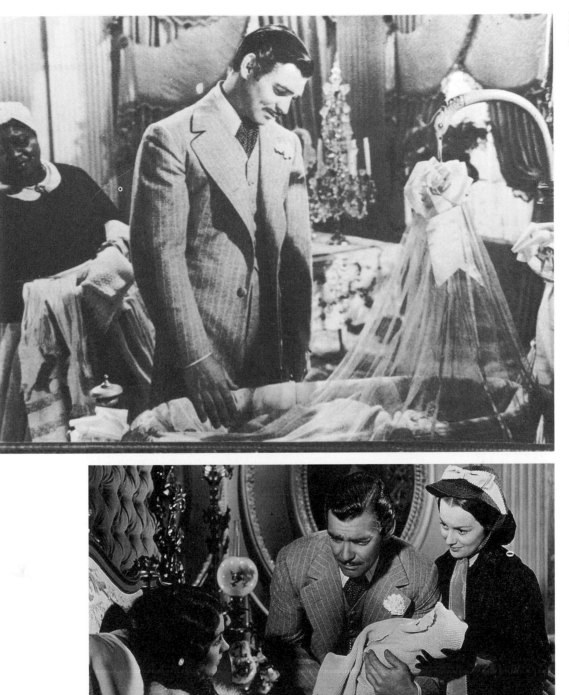

Mammy and Rhett admire the new baby.

Scarlett, Rhett, Melanie, and the baby, Eugenie Victoria. Her father, however, calls her Bonnie Blue, after a popular Confederate song, "Bonnie Blue Flag," and everyone else follows suit.

Scarlett in bed after the birth of Bonnie.

A publicity photograph of Olivia de Havilland as Melanie.

Scarlett, afraid pregnancy has ruined her figure, has Mammy check her waist measurement.

Facing page. It looks like a tender moment between Rhett and Scarlett— but she's holding a daguerreotype of Ashley in her left hand.

A production photograph of Ernest Haller and Vivien Leigh as they prepare to film the scene where Scarlett tells Rhett she won't sleep with him anymore.

A wardrobe still of Scarlett in costume for the No More Babies scene.

Leaving in a rage, Rhett kicks the door open. In the book Captain Butler leaves more quietly.

Rhett's bedroom in their Atlanta mansion. In a moment he will rush in, pour himself a drink, then hurl the glass at the portrait of Scarlett. This painting, by movie artist Helen Carlton, now hangs in an elementary-school auditorium in Atlanta.

Rhett seeks solace at Belle's.

A publicity photo of Ona Munson as Belle Watling. Notice the bells dangling from her ears and tiara. When the movie was made, Belle was a very "controversial, provocative" role, as Miss Munson said in an interview in *The Atlanta Journal.* She went on: "A number of people have asked me about my accent in the picture. Actually, Belle was in my conception a woman who had knocked about the world and I felt she would be played without too pronounced speech mannerisms, but with a husky, 'whiskey' voice."

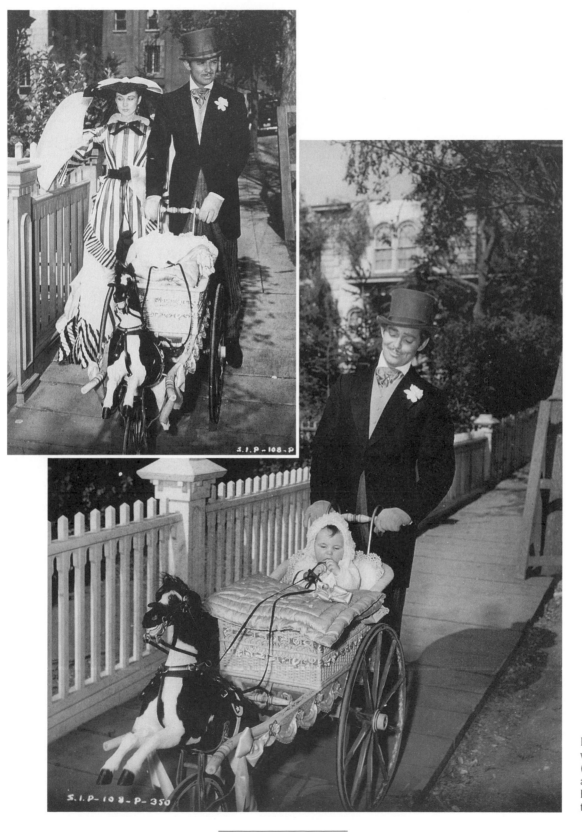

Scarlett and Rhett take Bonnie for a stroll down Peachtree Street.

S.I.P-108-P

S.I.P-108-P-350

Proud papa with Bonnie (Julie Tuck), already with her hands on the reins.

Vivien Leigh and Clark Gable on the set of Peachtree Street.

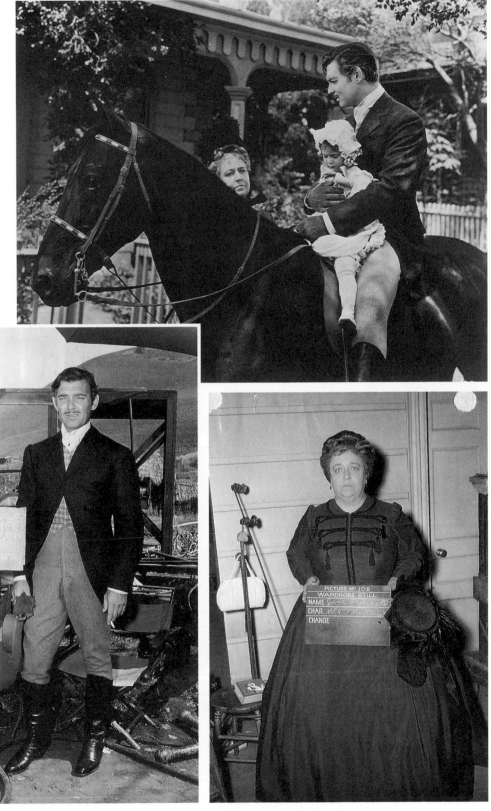

Rhett, anxious to make good in society for his daughter's sake, and Bonnie (Phyllis Callow) stop to chat with Mrs. Merriwether. They soon charm the imperious expression right off her face.

A wardrobe still of Rhett in his riding outfit.

A wardrobe still of Jane Darwell as Dolly Merriwether.

Rhett teaches Bonnie (Cammie King) to jump her pony. Cammie's older sister was originally slated for this role, but by the time they got to filming it, she had grown too big and Cammie took her place.

Cammie King gets a riding lesson from trainer Dick Smith. The horse is Bobby, a thoroughbred Shetland pony.

Clark Gable and Victor Fleming go over the script during a break in filming.

Scarlett visits Ashley at the lumber office; thinking back on old times at Twelve Oaks, they indulge in a comforting embrace.

A wardrobe
still of Ashley
in his
lumber-mill
costume.

A publicity
photograph of
Scarlett in
her mill-
visiting
costume.

Mrs. Meade and India find Scarlett in Ashley's arms.

Rhett, angered by the incident at the lumber mill, chooses a provocative dress for Scarlett to wear to Ashley's birthday party that evening. "Nothing modest or matronly will do for this occasion," he storms. "And put on plenty of rouge."

Preparing the scene where Scarlett dresses for the birthday party. A hairdresser checks Vivien's tresses; James Potevin, chief electrician is behind her, and Ernest Haller stoops near his camera.

Orchestra conductor Walter Damrosch visits Vivien on the set.

Melanie, Ashley, and Aunt Pittypat, and their guests at the party.

A wardrobe still of Ashley is his birthday costume.

A wardrobe still of Dr. Meade in his party outfit. The paper cup was not part of the costume.

Scarlett and Rhett in front of Melanie's house. He makes her go in alone.

Cast and crew celebrate Olivia de Havilland's birthday on the set of Ashley's Birthday Party. Victor Fleming appears to be directing the cake cutting. Script girl Lydia Schiller is in the striped shirt behind him. The cake reads, "Melanie—The Gang Wishes You A Happy Birthday."

Walter in his office with the plumes, fabric, and sketch for the dress.

Walter Plunkett's original watercolor of Scarlett's party dress.

173

David Selznick, Vivien Leigh, and Victor Fleming on the set. A studio caption describes the dress: "...a striking gown of burgundy velvet ornamented with scattered garnets and trimmed with wine-colored ostrich tips, which extend to the hem. A veil of wine tulle and three-quarter-length gloves of the same color; garnets in gold mountings for bracelet and earrings complete the ensemble."

Olivia entertains visitors to the set: Mrs. William T. Hopper of the United Daughters of the Confederacy (center) and Mrs. Wilbur Kurtz, whose husband was the production historian.

The interior of the Butlers' Atlanta mansion, which Scarlett herself has decorated with lots of money and little taste. As Margaret Mitchell wrote: "She thought it the most beautiful and most elegantly furnished house she had ever seen, but Rhett said it was a nightmare." Here Scarlett can be seen on the stairs as she descends in search of her husband.

In the dining room, an already drunk Rhett pours Scarlett a drink.

Vivien Leigh relaxes on the dining-room set.

Rhett takes Scarlett by the shoulders, just before he takes her up to the bedroom.

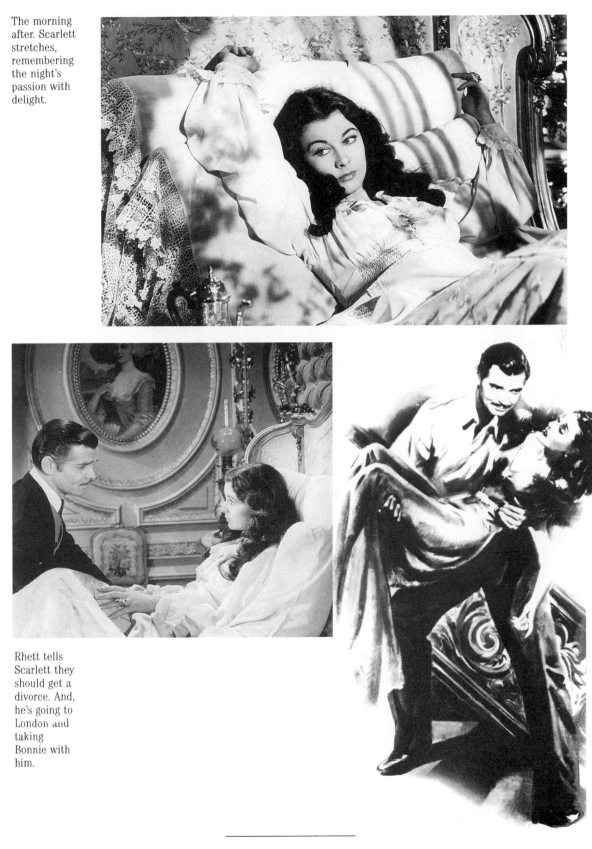

The morning after. Scarlett stretches, remembering the night's passion with delight.

Rhett tells Scarlett they should get a divorce. And, he's going to London and taking Bonnie with him.

A publicity painting of Rhett carrying Scarlett upstairs. "This is one night you're not turning me out," he vows.

Beau Wilkes (Mickey Kuhn) plays on the floor as Rhett talks to Bonnie.

A charming publicity photo of Rhett and Bonnie.

A publicity portrait of Cammie King as Bonnie Blue Butler.

A wardrobe still of Bonnie; but the board she's holding identifies her as Scarlett. Notice the doll clutched in the crook of her arm.

Bonnie, who is afraid of the dark, awakens screaming in the dark hotel room and is comforted by her father.

The nurse (Lillian Kemble Cooper) who should not have let the light go out; Rhett and Bonnie in the London hotel room.

A wardrobe still of Bonnie's nurse.

Cammie entertains herself with a tea set between takes.

Hattie McDaniel and some unidentified visitors on the set.

Bonnie, returned from London, is embraced by her mother. The child is holding a beribboned kitten.

Scarlett and Rhett have argued; she turns and falls down the stairs.

Scarlett unconscious at the bottom of the staircase.

The famous crying scene. Melanie comforts Rhett: "Scarlett loves you a great deal—much more than she knows."

Scarlett, recovering from her fall, and Rhett watch Bonnie ride the pony.

A publicity photo of Bonnie, in her blue velvet riding habit, and Bobby, the pony.

Bonnie, attempting a jump, has fallen from the pony and broken her neck. Rhett clutches his daughter's lifeless body to his breast.

Mammy informs Melanie of Rhett's grief-crazed behavior.

Melanie, having collapsed after helping Rhett through his sorrow, lies on her deathbed while the family waits in the parlor for word from Dr. Meade.

A wardrobe still of Rhett in the outfit he wears during Melanie's final hours.

A wardrobe still of Vivien Leigh in her costume for Melanie's Death.

Dr. Meade warns Scarlett not to make any last-minute confession as she enters Melly's bedroom.

A publicity photo of Laura Hope Crews as Aunt Pittypat.

THE FILMING

(Continued from page 57)

Fleming, who had raced cars, flown planes, and hunted tigers in earlier times of his life, was a brusque, brisk, macho type with a reputation as a "man's director."

This was in direct contrast with the intimate, introspective "women's director" style of Cukor. Softer, thoughtful, beneficent, George had forged a trust between Vivien, Olivia, and himself that the ladies tearfully begged Selznick to renew. But to no avail. Fleming was the director now, and that was that.

At least that's what Selznick thought. Once again Scarlett's wiles came to the forefront of Vivien's personality. On Sunday afternoons while Gable was dallying with Carole Lombard or dashing around town in his Dusenberg, Vivien was secretly ensconced at Cukor's house, going over her lines and motivations with the director she trusted.

Olivia, too, was coming to Cukor for clandestine advice, although the two women only rarely bumped into each other.

On the set, Vivien and Fleming had frequent spats, with the actress constantly consulting a battered copy of the book, and Fleming and Selznick fuming at her to put the damn thing away and do the scene as directed.

Gable serenely ignored all this, until the day came when it was his turn to be under the gun.

Filming reached the point where the script called for Gable to collapse in tears because Scarlett, goaded by Rhett, had fallen down the stairs, miscarried a child, and almost died.

Gable refused to cry on camera. He feared it would ruin his image with his fans, for in his mind (and in the popular culture of the day), real men did not cry.

Carole Lombard reminded him that he had always known it was in the script. Victor Fleming—a he-man among men himself—assured him the public would approve. But Gable was obstinate.

Finally Fleming told him they'd film two versions of the scene—one with tears, one without. Gable could review them both and have the final decision on which would be used. The actor reluctantly agreed.

Monday, May 29. A dim and rain-soaked light shadowed Gable's haggard face. There was absolute silence on the set. Then the sound of Melanie's gentle voice rose, and Rhett wept, wrenchingly, in full view of the camera. The scene was played beautifully, and even Gable was forced to agree that the tears should stay.

At the end of April, Fleming turned prima donna himself, storming off the set and refusing to come back, claiming he'd had a nervous breakdown. It took two weeks and a cage of lovebirds delivered to his Malibu beach house by Leigh, Gable, and Selznick to lure him back.

While he was gone, Selznick hired director number three for the picture: Sam Wood, a competent veteran of numerous other films. With Flemings' return, he decided to make the most of the situation, retaining Wood to work on one scene in the morning while Victor tackled another in the afternoon.

It was Fleming who filmed the memorable sequence in which Scarlett picks her way through hundreds of wounded soldiers outside the train station.

Selznick had planned this as a panoramic spectacle encompassing the bodies of every extra in Hollywood, but he ran into difficulties. First, there weren't nearly enough extras available—he wanted two thousand and only eight hundred answered the call. He decided to use dummies to fill in the gaps. Then the extras' guild insisted on being paid for the work the dummies would be doing.

Selznick haughtily refused, and on Monday, May 22, eight hundred extras, clothed in bloody, tattered uniforms, lay groaning in the sun, each man furtively manipulating a dummy lying at his feet or side.

To capture the desired effect, a special crane was hired, tall enough to lift the camera eighty-five feet into the air. This allowed the grandiose pullback shot, where Scarlett is seen surrounded by ever more bodies as the camera draws higher and farther away.

Fleming had earlier directed the scene where Scarlett runs through the congestion of evacuating Peachtree Street, dodging horses, wagons, and ambulances with reckless determination.

Vivien refused a double for this sequence, which she later described as "not a pleasant experience to see a gun caisson charging down on you—even when you know the riders are experts and the whole thing planned." [The sequence] "could not be done all in one continuous take, and so for what seemed like an eternity I dodged through the maze of traffic on Peachtree Street, timing myself to avoid galloping horses and thundering wagons. . . . I was so intent on being in the right place at the right time all day that I did not realize until I got to bed that night that Scarlett O'Hara Leigh was a badly bruised person."

Gable learned about exhaustion when Fleming directed the sequence where Rhett carries a kicking Scarlett up the long flight of stairs to the bedroom. Filming started late in the afternoon, and the scene had to be repeated over and over, until, as Vivien Leigh recalled, "even the stalwart Mr. Gable was beginning to feel it."

Finally Fleming called for one more take. The exhausted Gable picked up Vivien and trod the staircase yet again. "Thanks, Clark," Fleming said. "I really didn't need that shot—I just had a little bet on that you couldn't make it."

Melanie lies dying. But before she goes, she makes Scarlett promise to look after Ashley. And, she tells her, "Captain Butler—be kind to him. He loves you so."

Walter Plunkett's costume sketch for Scarlett's mourning gown in Melanie's Death scene.

Scarlett runs through the mist in a repetition of her recurring nightmare in which she is always searching in the fog for something or someone— she now knows it was Rhett and that she loves him.

He is packing a suitcase, planning to leave her. Scarlett tells him she loves him but he doesn't believe her.

At home, Scarlett finds Rhett sitting in his bedroom.

Selznick, Fleming, Leigh, and Gable on the set for the final scenes of the film. Surprisingly, of all the hundreds of production stills taken by the studio during filming of the movie, none were made of the climactic scene where Rhett walks out the door, leaving Scarlett standing staring after him in tears.

CHAPTER FOUR

Post-
PRODUCTION

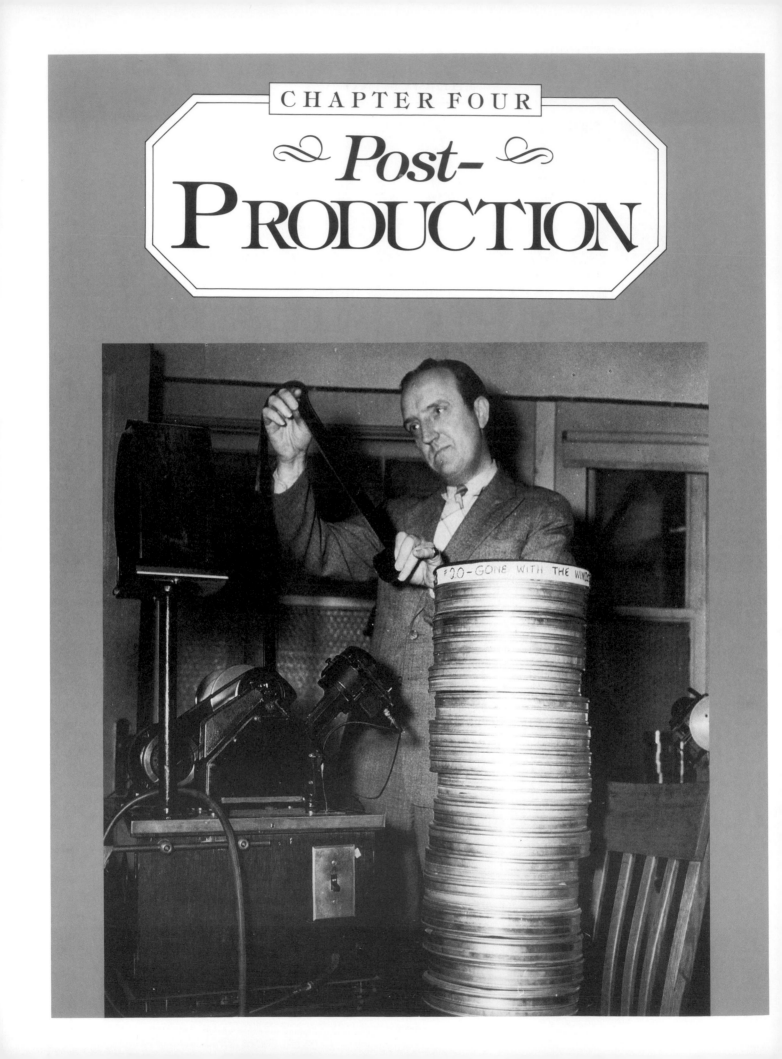

All through filming, Selznick was still tinkering with the script. He desperately wanted to show Rhett engaged in blockade-running and Ashley heroically battling the Yankees. "I feel it is important," he noted in an intra-studio memo, "to see both of these characters who stand around during most of the picture doing so much talking in action scenes." At the end of June, five months into shooting, he was still attempting to work in a montage of cavalry charges, sword fights, and gunplay featuring Ashley Wilkes.

Leslie Howard really was an excellent horseman, having been an officer in the British Cavalry, and Selznick was convinced this would add to Ashley's onscreen glory. Thomas Mitchell, on the other hand, was a direct contrast to his character, Gerald O'Hara, where horses were concerned. Although Gerald delighted in tearing around on a fast mount, leaping over fences, he was terrified of horses and sat on one only after Fleming bullied him into it.

Leslie Howard's horse, Rebel, was a star in his own right. So was Rhett Butler's mount, Black Chief, "the screen name of Alexander Twigg, once a famous mid-western show horse," according to publicity. If there was a class system among the

(Continued on page 196)

After Rhett leaves, Scarlett returns to Tara. This version of the last scene in the film was deleted from the final film. As with the dramatic scene where Rhett walks away, no production stills were made of the famous final pullback shot of Scarlett silhouetted against the Tara sunset.

S.I.P-108

Upon completion of filming, a cast party was held on the set. Having a good time here are David Selznick, Vivien Leigh, Victor Fleming, Carole Lombard, and Clark Gable.

Editing the voluminous reels of film. Left to right: Richard Von Enger (Assistant Film Editor), James E. Newcom (Associate Film Editor), Hal Kern, Jr., and Stuart Frye. Notice the hefty script atop one stack of film cans.

Vivien Leigh
and her
Hollywood
secretary,
Sunny
Alexander.

Supervising
Film Editor
Hal Kern
with the
completed
movie "in the
can."

Max Steiner conducts the symphony orchestra used to score the film. The studio caption adds: "His score is one of the longest and most dramatic and beautiful ever written for motion pictures."

(Continued from page 193)

animals on the picture, Black Chief surely reigned at the pinnacle, and beneath him were 1,000 horses and 375 other assorted beasts, including dogs, mules, oxen, cows, pigs, chickens, ducks, geese, and peacocks.

The studio fact sheet detailing these animal statistics lists "9,000 bit and extra people" in between the horses and the dogs, mules, etc. It is odd that human actors were acknowledged this way, though they were given credit ahead of the 450 assorted vehicles: wagons, hearses, fire equipment, carriages, ambulances, and gun caissons.

A different type of vehicle, a trailer replete with dressing room, was used to transport cast and crew to Lasky Mesa, sixty miles outside the studio in the Simi Valley, for the filming of Scarlett's retching over a radish and vowing to "never be hungry again." Vivien Leigh, Victor Flem-

ing and the necessary camera, and makeup and crew people had already made this trip half a dozen times, hoping to catch a properly scenic sunrise.

Finally, on May 23, having left the studio at eleven P.M. after a full day's shooting, they drove north to Lasky Mesa yet again, arriving in time to capture a picture-perfect dawn on film. Perhaps this was more luck than timing, for according to Vivien Leigh in the souvenir program, "The sun rose shortly after two A.M.," surely an unheard-of hour for sunrise anywhere south of the Arctic Circle.

But the sun, and Vivien, performed admirably, and the group returned home at four-thirty, just in time for an hour's sleep before reporting to the studio again.

"Yet I do not recall that I was so terribly tired," Vivien reported. "Instead I think of
(Continued on page 204)

Lou Forbes, head of the studio music department, consults the score with Max Steiner.

A hairdresser puts the finishing touch on Vivien's hair before the photograph is taken. As Scarlett, she wore 38 different hairstyles during the course of the film.

A series of publicity photographs were made by famed Hollywood photographer Clarence Bull:

Rhett and Scarlett in a rapturous moment. Clarence Bull stands to the right with his hand around the camera button.

Mr. Bull's finished photographs.

Facing page. Scarlett is in the dress she wears to walk Bonnie in her carriage.

Rhett, and Scarlett in the burgundy gown.

Ann Rutherford, the first of the Hollywood stars to arrive in Atlanta, is met at the train station by Mayor Hartsfield (standing next to Ann with hat in hand).

Atlanta mayor William B. Hartsfield presents a bouquet of roses to Mrs. Howard Dietz (the former Lady Guiniss of London). Her husband, stepping down from the train behind her, was the head of MGM's advertising and publicity department.

Olivia de Havilland; David Selznick; his wife, Irene; and Vivien Leigh are greeted at the Atlanta airport by Mayor Hartsfield. Note the fellow in period costume at the right of the photo.

Chief of Police M. A. Hornsby (left) and Miss Emily Claire Millican of Atlanta (right) present flowers to Ona Munson and Evelyn Keyes.

201

Orchestra leader Kay Kyser, Carole Lombard, and Clark Gable, just arrived on American Airlines' Sky Sleeper, are greeted by Georgia Governor Ed Rivers. The airlines sent a special representative along on the flight to make sure the stars were properly taken care of.

Vivien Leigh smiles out from between David Selznick and John Jay (Jock) Whitney. Governor Rivers is in the front seat.

Clark Gable, Carole Lombard, and Mayor Hartsfield perch atop a Lincoln Zephyr convertible during the parade of stars through downtown Atlanta. The mayor had declared a citywide half-day holiday for the event.

The parade winds through cheering crowds along Peachtree Street. Vivien Leigh, hearing bands playing "Dixie" along the route, cried out, "They're playing the music from the picture!"

(Continued from page 196)
the day that Scarlett shoots the deserter ...after that nerve-wracking episode, both Olivia de Havilland...and myself were on the verge of hysterics—not alone from the tenseness of the scene, but from the all too real fall as the 'dead' man went down the stairs before us."

By the time filming of *Gone With the Wind* was officially completed on July 1, Vivien had good reason to be not merely tired but exhausted. She had worked 125 days, or five months, with only a few days off during the entire ordeal. In contrast, Gable worked 71 days, Olivia 59, and Leslie Howard only 32.

It was apparent to most observers that Vivien Leigh was driving herself at top speed, and harder than Scarlett drove her sisters to pick cotton after the war. Feverish with desire to finish the movie and fly to New York and Olivier, *GWTW*'s leading lady threw herself into the project with a disregard for rest of any kind.

At last the day came when the final scene was to be filmed—Scarlett sobbing on the staircase for the departed Rhett. Vivien had had to postpone her New York flight for this scene, a last-minute invention of Selznick's, and as a consequence, the tears were real.

Selznick himself had had a terrible time with this scene. Sidney Howard's screenplay (and all subsequent versions) ended the way the novel did, with Rhett leaving Scarlett alone and despondent in the huge, ornate house. But the script gave no hint, as Margaret Mitchell did in her book, that "She knew she could get [Rhett] back. There had never been a man she couldn't get, once she set her mind to it."

Selznick felt the script version ended on a "terribly depressing note," and he cast about desperately for some way to give the movie's finale a more upbeat quality. Finally he hit on the idea of having the "ghostly" voices of Gerald, Rhett, and Ashley remind Scarlett of her love for Tara and the land. The scene would then cut from the distraught Scarlett on the stairs to a brave Scarlett silhouetted against the flaming backdrop of Tara. This would echo a lighter, warmer exchange between the girl and her father early in the film, when they discuss their love of the land and also would give the ending the necessary uplift.

Another Selznick touch was the addition of a single word to a sentence written by Margaret Mitchell—one word that so changed the line that it achieved instant immortality. In the novel, Rhett answers Scarlett's question of "...if you go, what shall I do?" with "My dear, I don't give a damn."

David affixed the word *frankly* to the beginning of the line, a simple addition that imbued the phrase with a rhythm and a chilling indifference that didn't exist before. Clark Gable's reading of the line gives it the electric thrill that sent it into history, but he had to record two different versions: *frankly* wasn't the problem, *damn* was.

The Hays Office was a board of movie censors that had been established in the early 1930s as a counterattack to all the naughty ladies in silk tap pants and bleached hair spreading immorality across American movie screens. And like many watchdog committees, the Hays people tended to err on the side of justice, zealously protecting moviegoers from such prurient times as double beds (even among the married), childbirth, and profanity, including the heinous word *damn*.

As a precaution against the whims of the Hays Office, Rhett Butler read his famous line once as "Frankly, my dear, I don't care," and again, with the *damn* left in.

David Selznick then went to bat for the taboo version, arguing, "The omission of this line spoils the punch at the very end of the picture and on our very fade-out gives an impression of unfaithfulness...to Miss Mitchell's work...."

The Hays Office, like most everyone else in Hollywood, could not withstand the gale force of David Selznick on a roll and eventually gave in. *Gone With the Wind* was given the seal of approval, and the added fillip
(Continued on page 209)

Thousands of fans choke the streets in front of the Georgian Terrace Hotel, "*GWTW* Head-quarters," and end of the parade route.

A platform was erected in front of the hotel so the stars could greet their fans. Notice the newsreel camera perched on its own little platform above the crowd and the flag bunting draped along the street.

The Georgia State Girls Military Band plays for the crowd and celebrities in front of the hotel. The Fox Theater can be seen across the street.

Clark Gable says a few words to the fans.

Vivien Leigh, Clark Gable, and Olivia de Havilland are shown through Atlanta's famous cyclorama of the Battle of Atlanta by George Simons, City Parks Manager. Tourists are not ordinarily allowed to walk through the display, but an exception was made for Hollywood.

POST-PRODUCTION

Margaret Mitchell (center) is surrounded by Vivien Leigh, Clark Gable, David Selznick, and Olivia de Havilland at the Piedmont Driving Club. This was Miss Mitchell's first meeting with the stars.

Vivien Leigh, Laurence Olivier, and David and Irene Selznick arrive for the Junior League Ball at the Atlanta Municipal Auditorium. Mr. Olivier, press and publicity all insisted, was in Atlanta "on his own business."

A studio publicity photo of Vivien Leigh in the gown Walter Plunkett designed for her to wear to the *GWTW* Ball.

Clark Gable,
Carole
Lombard,
Mayor
Hartsfield
and his
daughter
Mildred
arrive at the
Ball.

David
Selznick and
Vivien Leigh
in their box
seat at the
Ball.
Claudette
Colbert is
just behind
them, to the
right. "Poor
deluded
Claudette,"
Selznick had
commented
earlier, "is
coming [to
Atlanta]
under the
notion that
she is going
to have a
good time."

Millie Hartsfield shares a confidence with Gable. Her father is seated just behind them.

(Continued from page 204)
of barely sanctioned wickedness.

Now that shooting was complete, there came the still grueling work of post-production.

The first order of business, and the biggest problem, was editing. Counting every frame that had been filmed, the movie ran just under six hours. Selznick and film editor, Hal Kern, spent two long months, including some marathon forty-eight-hour shifts, running the footage through Movieola projectors, trying to decide what to leave in and what to take out.

Some of the scenes that fell by the wayside were a sequence showing the slaves enjoying their own barbecue at Twelve Oaks; Scarlett's wedding night with the doomed Charles Hamilton; various shots of the dance at the bazaar; a sequence (not in the book) with Belle Watling giving wa-

ter to the wounded; Belle and her ladies on the stand at an inquiry into Frank Kennedy's murder; and the death of Ashley's father, John Wilkes.

A proposed (and already written) scene showing another John Wilkes—the John Wilkes Booth who killed Lincoln—at the theater never materialized. Nor did any of Selznick's dreamed-of cavalry sequences, making *Gone With the Wind* the only Civil War movie without a single battle scene. The "Burning of Atlanta" was considerably shortened, and a segment was added showing Scarlett, her horse, wagon, and its frail human cargo huddled under a bridge on the way home to Tara after passing through the inferno.

The Hall Johnson Choir had been hired to sing as they worked in the cotton fields at the beginning of the picture. A few establishing shots of Tara, green and gold under the Georgia sun, were filmed by a second unit in Chico, a farming region in northern California, and spliced in around the choir.

Cammie King, the child who played Bonnie Blue Butler, had been carefully schooled to jump a real pony and her scenes duly filmed. But during editing, Selznick decided he didn't like her voice and had all her lines dubbed by another actress.

Marcella (Cathleen Calvert) Martin's lines were dubbed, too, on the grounds that she didn't sound Southern enough—even though she was from the South.

For the film's score Selznick hired Max Steiner, a rotund Viennese with whom he had worked before (notably on *King Kong*).

The movie premiere had been promised to the city of Atlanta by mid-December, and time was running out. Steiner wanted this assignment, but he had a tendency to panic, frequently complaining that he couldn't possibly complete the lengthy work in the time allotted to him. But each time he threatened to quit, Selznick would counter with a threat to put another composer on the job and Steiner would climb back into harness.

Despite his fears, he finished in time, having wrought a magnificent score—a richly sweeping, emotionally variegated orchestration that includes separate themes for Scarlett, Rhett, Melanie, and, of course, Tara itself.

Now Selznick decided he needed a grandly orchestrated opening sequence to match. Hal Kern came up with the idea of the words *Gone With the Wind* sweeping across the screen, and David penned the lead-in phrases: " . . . a land of Cavaliers and Cotton Fields called the Old South. Look for it only in books . . . for it is a Civilization gone with the wind."

The movie had been prodded, primped, and primed down to four and a half hours; edited, cut, and coddled through dubbing, inserts, and deletions. It was time to preview it before an audience.

A weekday evening in early September. Selznick had entrusted Hal Kern with the job of getting he, his wife, studio backer Jock Whitney, and the twenty-four cans of film to a local theater in absolute secrecy. This was to be an unannounced screening, and he cautioned Kern not to tell a soul where it was going to be held.

Kern was well acquainted with Selznick's ways. Realizing that David was the only one who couldn't be trusted to keep his mouth shut, Kern steadfastly refused to tell him the location. He merely arranged for a car to pick up the Selznicks and travel to a theater location only the driver would know.

The manager of the lucky theater, two hours away in Riverside, had not been forewarned. But when Kern got out of the car, staggering under the weight of his twenty-four film cans, the manager guessed what was going on and insisted on calling his wife.

Kern allowed him, like a prisoner in a precinct house, only the one phone call, during which he was permitted to tell her to get right down to the theater, but not the reason why.

Then the movie audience was told that a special preview would be shown instead of the movie normally scheduled, that it was very long, and anyone wishing to leave the theater would have to do so immediately. Once the screening began, the doors would be locked and no one permitted to enter, leave, or make phone calls.

The theater patrons, sensing something special, settled back, ready for a treat. When the title *Gone With the Wind* flashed across the screen, the audience rose to its collective feet, cheering, applauding, and screaming. Jock Whitney and Irene Selznick burst into tears. And when the movie was over, the standing ovation was repeated in its entirety.

A few days later another surprise preview was held, this time in Santa Barbara, two hours to the north. Here, too, the film was greeted with thunderous applause.

Back at the studio, Selznick poured over the preview cards, which moviegoers had filled out after each screening. The general consensus, and the phrase that leaped out from card after card, was "the greatest picture I've ever seen."

Selznick was delighted, but work still remained to be done. Four and a half hours was still too long, and he, Kern, and Fleming set to work re-editing, cutting snips and bits here and there, and adding in a few more bridging scenes.

This done, the film was shown—with great trepidation on Selznick's part—to the MGM executives, who loved it as much as the Riverside and Santa Barbara audiences had. But the fact that it had to be interrupted in several spots so Louis B. Mayer could use the men's room convinced Selznick to add an intermission. The film had now reached its final length of three hours and forty-five minutes.

Now came the credits. Although the movie had had countless writers and David Selznick claimed credit for a great deal of the script himself, he decided to give screen credit to Sidney Howard. Partly this was because Howard had done the original work on the project, especially distilling the plot, and partly as a tribute to the departed. Howard had been killed in a tractor accident on his farm a month before the first screening and never saw the movie to which he had contributed so much.

Selznick had mulled over the idea of giving directorial credit to George Cukor and Sam Wood, along with Victor Fleming. But when he suggested it to Fleming, it was met as a tremendous insult. Victor felt that he had put by far the most work into the picture (which was true) and that it was his alone. Selznick dropped the matter and Fleming's name appeared on the screen as the only director.

There had also been a great deal of discussion over whose name to put before the movie's title—Clark Gable as the male lead, Vivien Leigh as the female, or some combination thereof. Selznick put an end to this by declaring that only one name belonged at the beginning of the picture—Margaret Mitchell. And that is precisely what was done.

And the movie was now ready for the big time. Lights, action, Atlanta!

CHAPTER FIVE

The PREMIERE!

THE PREMIERE!

The city of Atlanta was in a frenzy of excitement. Hollywood was coming to town!

And not just for any old reason but for the premiere of *Gone With the Wind*, the picture the entire nation was waiting to see—a picture written by a local author about Atlanta and Atlantans. This would be the social event of the century.

Three full days of festivities were planned, beginning on Wednesday, December 13, and culminating with the movie premiere itself on Friday evening. Balls were organized; teas, benefits, parties, parades, and concerts arranged; radio programs, marching bands, drill teams, and musical entertainments whipped into shape.

Newspapers heralded the approaching activities for months in advance, devoting front-page full-column space and headlines as premiere day drew near.

Merchants used the event as a springboard for tie-in advertising. Davison-Paxon, Atlanta's finest department store, ran a half-page ad for evening formals to rival Scarlett's, from $10.95 to $17.95, and its street-level book department proudly featured the yellow-jacketed novel.

Davison's, which now flies under the Macy's banner, shared a bit of history with *GWTW*. It had been one of the first stores to sell the book when it first came out in 1936. Margaret Mitchell had presented an autographed copy (something she rarely did) to Colonel Paxon, the store's owner and an old family friend. The colonel looked down at the fat volume and handed it right back to its author. His only comment: "Margaret, that damn book is too heavy."

Davison-Paxon, along with the majority of Atlanta merchants, had mixed feelings about the premiere. They were, of course, delighted with the advertising opportunities but unhappy about the timing. David Selznick originally had promised that the movie would be available in September, then November, and now here it finally was in December—just in time for the Christmas rush, when they didn't need the advertising bonus. It would have been more financially beneficial earlier in the year.

But no one turns his back on a good deal, no matter when it comes, and store owners, restauranteurs, even taxicab companies, joined the common citizenry in embracing the event with open arms.

Henry McLemore, a United Press correspondent, wrote in an article carried in *The Atlanta Journal*, "I've covered many a spectacle in many a country—the Olympic Games in Berlin, the Grand Prix in Paris ...but I have never seen a city give itself so completely to one thing as Atlanta has to the movie premiere of...*Gone With the Wind.*"

Selznick International had generously sent ahead various costumes for the movie for merchants to use in adorning their win-

Facing page. The night of nights. Loew's Grand Theatre on Peachtree Street in a blaze of light for the big premiere.

LOEW'S GRAND THEATRE
World Premiere of
GONE WITH THE WIND
Sponsored by the
ATLANTA COMMUNITY FUND
Friday, December 15, 1939 • 8:15 p. m.
Admission Price: Ten Dollars per ticket
Tax Exempt

ORCHESTRA
Loew's Grand Theatre
Friday Evening, Dec. 15, 1939
CENTR
CC101

A ticket to the world premiere of *Gone With the Wind.*

Ona Munson speaks into a radio microphone in front of the theater.

dows. Those not fortunate enough to get hold of these precious items decorated their storefronts with antebellum dresses, Confederate bills; yellowing, ink-stained letters from Rebel generals, and giant cardboard replicas of Rhett kissing Scarlett.

Waitresses and cabdrivers went about their duties in hoopskirts and peg-top pants, while bartenders served up Scarlett cocktails and newspapermen prowled the streets.

The main order of events was to be the arrival of half the movie contingent, beginning with Ann Rutherford and leading up to Olivia de Havilland and Vivien Leigh on Wednesday; the arrival of the other (and more wildly exciting) half, Clark Gable and Carole Lombard, on Thursday; followed by a parade through the streets, a radio address, and the Junior League costume ball. Then on Friday, after a flurry of minor festivities, would come the grand premiere.

Wednesday morning found Atlanta's mayor, William B. Hartsfield, down at the train station at eight-twenty-five sharp to greet Howard Dietz, head of MGM adver-

Vivien Leigh waves to the crowd as she enters the theater. Obscured here by fox fur, her gown is another stunning Walter Plunkett creation, gold lamé with a harem hemline and draped girdle studded with gold sequins. Laurence Olivier can be seen at the right of the photo.

THE PREMIERE!

Hollywood's glamour couple—Carole Lombard and Clark Gable—in front of the Loew's Grand.

Margaret Mitchell turns to go into the theater.

Inside the theater at last, waiting for the lights to go down. Front row, left to right, are: Leonard Bames Swopes; Claudette Colbert; Mrs. Ed Rivers and her husband, the governor; Vivien Leigh. Second row: Olivia de Havilland; Jock Whitney; Margaret Mitchell; her husband, John Marsh; Clark Gable; Carole Lombard; Mayor Hartsfield and Millie.

tising and publicity, and his wife. Mayor Hartsfield presented the missus with a bouquet of red roses and gave the couple a siren-screaming police escort to the Georgian Terrace Hotel, the most elegant hotel in town, and *Gone With the Wind* headquarters.

At ten A.M., the mayor was back at the train station to greet Ann Rutherford (Carreen O'Hara) and her mother, present another bouquet, and provide another police escort.

Miss Rutherford, Mickey Rooney's girlfriend in a string of popular Andy Hardy films and the first "movie star" to arrive on Atlanta soil, was met with cheers from an adoring crowd, popping newspaper flashbulbs, and Movietone newsreel cameras.

At three-thirty that afternoon, the plane bearing Vivien Leigh, Olivia de Havilland, and David Selznick was only nineteen miles out from Candler Field and the TWA terminal. Brisk tail winds had brought it in forty-five minutes ahead of schedule, and

A rather sedate poster lists cast and crew.

Olivia de Havilland, Jock Whitney, Margaret Mitchell, and John Marsh exchange pleasantries in what must have been a nerve-racking interlude before the picture begins.

216

THE PREMIERE!

Paintings and posters decorate the lobby of Loew's Grand Theatre:

Original paintings based on the movie, flanked by silhouetted figures.

GONE WITH THE WIND
NEVER IN A LIFETIME HAVE
EYES BEHELD ITS EQUAL

The theater entrance. Notice the confident slogan below the film title.

217

Crowds queue up in front of the Astor Theatre for *GWTW*'s New York premiere. Notice the policeman on horseback near the center of the photo.

Another view of the Astor on premiere night. The electric sign running horizontally across "Gone With the Wind" reads: All Seats Reserved.

Mayor Hartsfield was in a panic. The ladies would arrive before their red-rose bouquets reached the airport by car.

Dashing up to the control tower, the mayor had the copilot contacted by radio. "Don't let them come in yet," he pleaded. "Tell the pilot to take them over Stone Mountain; I'm sure they'd like to see it."

The pilot complied and the stars landed, after their impromptu air tour, in a welter of luggage (ten cars were required for six people and their gear), furs, perfume, flashbulbs, and cheering fans.

Laura Hope Crews was to arrive by train the next day. Selznick had refused to let her come by plane, saying "Aunt Pittypat would never do that."

And there was the mayor at Union Station, awaiting the Dixie Limited from Chicago, at eighty-twenty Thursday morning. Next he was to dash to Terminal Station for Claudette Colbert's arrival at eight-twenty-five. (Claudette, a major star of the day, had nothing to do with the movie but thought she'd like to be in on the festivities, anyway.) Luckily for Mr. Hartsfield, Miss Crews's train was late, having been derailed somewhere along the way, and Miss Colbert decided to time her arrival for later in the afternoon. The mayor could take a breather.

It was three-thirty P.M., the moment all of Atlanta had been waiting for. American Airlines' Sky Sleeper from Los Angeles completed its fifteen-hour flight, drawing to earth Clark Gable and Carole Lombard.

The Russell High Military Band struck up a brisk tune, and the thirty-one members of the Blue Rainbow Girls Drill Team bounced into action. Mayor Hartsfield stepped forward with his flowers, and the contingent was loaded into cars for the parade into town.

Vivien, Olivia, Ann Rutherford, Laura Hope Crews, Ona Munson, Evelyn Keyes, and a bevy of studio executives had already been trooped out from the hotel to the airport to join the cavalcade.

Leslie Howard did not attend any of these premiere events. England had just entered World War II, and he had left Hollywood to enjoin the cause. Victor Fleming was not at the premiere, either, ostensibly due to the recent death of his great friend, Douglas Fairbanks, Sr., but possibly because he was still miffed at Selznick for suggesting he share directorial credits for the film.

But the movie people who did show up were more than enough for Atlanta. As Henry McLemore had written the day before, "All [Clark Gable] has to face [is] a parade through the heart of the city and a reception that is limited to half the voters of Georgia."

The big convertibles inched through streets choked with fans. *The Atlanta Journal* reported, "At Five Points [in the center of town] there were people, people, people as far as the eye could reach. It was a great and moving spectacle in the gathering dusk, with bits of paper cascading from the tall buildings and the roars of the crowd as the cars moved along a narrow path."

Arriving at last before the honey-colored stone facade of the Georgian Terrace, the cars released their celebrity passengers to the milling throng and onto the narrow veranda edging the hotel.

Here they were greeted by five marshals, the governors of five Southern states, the Junior Chamber of Commerce, the Red Rainbow Girls Drill team, the Georgia State Girls Military Band, and Bartlett and McMillan of radio station WSB in Atlanta, who would also broadcast another program later in the evening that would tie into the NBC national network of stations.

Following the introductions of celebrities and others, the raising of the Confederate flag by Clark Gable, a rendition of "Dixie" by the Girls Military Band, eleven salutes fired by a pyrotechnical expert, and the Star-Spangled Banner, the company was released into the warmth of the hotel ballroom for a cocktail party.

Then, after barely a breather, the stars were popped back into automobiles for a trip down Peachtree Street to the City Auditorium and the Junior League Ball.

Ann Rutherford and Tom Connors, Jr., in front of the Capitol Theatre for the New York premiere.

The auditorium was dressed to simulate the armory in the bazaar scene from the film. The Junior Leaguers and their guests were similarly attired, floating across the floor in rustling creations of chiffon and silk, ribbons and lace, recently unearthed from the mothballs of their grannies' attic trunks.

Streamers of smilax and laurel and Confederate flags festooned the building. Sets from the movie bazaar—courtesy of David Selznick—were ranged along the inside of the hall, while the facade of Twelve Oaks dominated the background. On the stage was the facade of Tara, replete with magnolias, boxwood, wisteria, and a real lawn reaching beyond the proscenium to the orchestra pit.

Kay Kyser, a popular bandleader who billed himself as Professor of the College of Musical Knowledge, headlined the event, and over at the Paramount—next door to the theater where the premiere would be held—Ozzie Nelson's orchestra played for those who could not get into the ball.

The mayor's twenty-year-old daughter, Millie, on an evening that probably ranked among the highest in her life, sat at Gable's right, while lovely Carole Lombard flanked him on the left.

Margaret Palmer, one of Atlanta's leading debs, won the honor of wearing Scarlett's green sprigged barbecue dress. She was the only one of her set, with measurements to match Vivien Leigh's, to properly fill the three-thousand-dollar costume.

Though six thousand dazzling, and dazzled, Atlantans attended the ball, it was nothing compared to the premiere the next night.

"The envy of every girl in Atlanta," according to *The Atlanta Journal*, "are four grizzled Confederate veterans from the Old Soldiers' Home who will see the premiere as guests of Clark Gable."

Henry McLemore of United Press interviewed one of these old fellows, 92-year-old J. A. Skelton, who had never seen a "moving picture." When asked how a Technicolor, talking, moving picture was going to affect him, he answered, "Son, it won't mean nothing to me. I've seen plenty of lantern slides."

Mr. Skelton was the exception to the rule.

Eighteen thousand excited souls crowded the streets, each vying for a glimpse of the stars as they rode the few miles from the hotel to the Loew's Grand Theater on Peachtree Street.

The entire affair must have been a great blow to the Fox Theater people. For the Fox Theater, an ornate movie palace in its own right, was (and still is) directly across the street from the Georgian Terrace Hotel. But as close as the Fox was to the "headquarters of *Gone With the Wind*" and all the attendant action, it might have been a million miles for all the ticket sales it could hope to achieve.

In the thirties, theaters, movies, and distribution companies were all corporately tied up together. A theater could not show a film distributed by a rival concern. The

Jack Haley (*The Wizard of Oz's* Tin Man) and Charlie Ruggles in the lobby of the Astor.

Tony Martin and Alice Faye just inside the Capitol.

Fox Theater in Atlanta was bound by contract to 20th Century-Fox films and could only sit back and watch all the lovely publicity and money parade away down the road to the Loew's, which was smartly affiliated with MGM.

The Loew's Grand did itself proud. The facade of Tara towered over the theater entrance. Above it, the faces of Scarlett and Rhett touched lips within an enormous full-color medallion. Spotlights were trained on the theater marquee, while the rays of five 800-million-candlepower searchlights probed the night sky, reportedly visible in Jasper, Georgia, sixty-five miles away.

Earlier that day, the stars enjoyed a tour of the Cyclorama, an Atlanta Civil War attraction; the governor's mansion, adorned with hundreds of electric holiday lights; and attended various teas and luncheons.

At the Women's Press Club fete, Margaret Mitchell met the living embodiment of Rhett Butler as she and Clark Gable closeted themselves in a private room for the better part of an hour. Both declined to say what the course of their conversation was, but each was obviously charmed by the other.

Then night fell over the city and the premiere hour drew near.

Outside the theater, crowd control was accomplished with the combined assistance of the city police, twelve firemen, fifty state troopers, four hundred National Guardsmen, and seven hundred Boy Scouts.

Inside the movie house, ushers and ticket takers were garbed in antebellum outfits, and *Gone With the Wind* posters and paintings decorated the walls.

Since the theater seated only 2,051 people, one had to have either uncommon connections or the guile of Scarlett O'Hara to get tickets. And then, one had to be able to afford the purchase price. A single ticket to

the premiere went for ten dollars, this at a time when the average evening box-office tab was fifty cents.

But even those who could not afford fifty cents could stand outside and watch Margaret Mitchell arrive decked out in pale pink tulle; Vivien Leigh, adorned in draped gold lamé; Olivia de Havilland in black velvet with black lace appliqués; Ona Munson in dark green velvet with a bustle; and Carole Lombard, all champagne satin, on the tuxedoed arm of Clark Gable. A thousand sighs went out from a thousand lips.

Once inside the theater, the audience settled back in a haze of expectancy muffled by fox furs, minks, and gold brocades.

Gable, at the microphone in the front of the theater, addressed the crowd: "Tonight I am here just as a spectator.... This is Margaret Mitchell's night and the people

Jimmy Stewart escorts Olivia de Havilland past banks of flowers at the Capitol. Irene Selznick can be seen at the left of the photo.

THE PREMIERE!

Burgess Meredith, ticket in hand, in the lobby of the Astor.

A gala crowd of "first-nighters" in the lobby of the Capitol. Note the spiffily uniformed usher in the foreground.

223

Barbara O'Neil with nosegay, and husband, Broadway producer Josh Logan, inside the Capitol.

Anita Loos, author of *Gentlemen Prefer Blondes*, and John Frederics in the lobby of the Capitol.

Radio commentator Walter Winchell and his daughter at the Capitol Theatre.

of Atlanta's night."

The stage went dark, the curtain went up, and Max Steiner's thrilling score flooded the theater.

The audience laughed and cried and cheered and cried again, in all the right places. The curtain came down and the lights came on to a round of thunderous applause. There wasn't a dry eye in the house.

Margaret Mitchell, the lady so averse to public recognition, took the stage. "It was a tremendous emotional experience for me," she said. "It's not up to me to speak of the grand things these actors have done.... I want to commend Mr. Selznick's courage and his obstinacy and his determination in just keeping his mouth shut until he got exactly the cast he wanted."

She summed up David Selznick in a nutshell, and the evening was summed up brilliantly. Her novel, Selznick's movie, and the work of every individual in the cast and crew produced a masterpiece.

The word went out on wire services, newsreels, and radio shows: *Gone With the Wind* was an overwhelming success.

Gimbel's store window all decked out with costumes and pictures from the movie.

Jock Whitney, Irene Selznick, Olivia de Havilland, David O. Selznick, Vivien Leigh, and Laurence Olivier in front of the Carthay Circle.

The last hurdle—the Hollywood premiere. Carole Lombard, Clark Gable, Marion Davies, and Raoul Walsh at the Carthay Circle Theatre in Los Angeles.

THE PREMIERE!

Walter
Plunkett
admires both
Ginger
Rogers and
the outfit he
designed for
her to wear to
the
Hollywood
premiere.

Claudette
Colbert and
husband
Dr. Joel
Pressman.

Mr. and Mrs.
Gene Autry.

Ann
Rutherford
and Rand
Brooks.

THE PREMIERE!

A glowing Hattie McDaniel arrives for the Hollywood premiere.

Fay Bainter presents Hattie McDaniel with the Academy Award for Best Actress in a Supporting Role.

A beaming David Selznick helps Vivien Leigh show off her Best Actress Oscar.

CHAPTER SIX
The
PHENOMENON

THE PHENOMENON

As the empty theater settled back into darkness with only the echoes of applause sounding in the rafters, the stars caught planes and trains for home, and movie critics raced to meet the morning-edition deadline.

The reviews were unanimously favorable. Lee Rodgers, of *The Atlanta Constitution*, opened his column with a one-sentence paragraph: "It is wonderful." He went on to add: "*Gone With the Wind* opens a new film era. It has everything a great picture could have. It has everything that everybody wanted.

"Vivien Leigh is 'Scarlett.' And Clark Gable is now, more so than ever, the box office public's choice as 'Rhett Butler.' "

Over at *The Atlanta Journal*, Frank Daniel wrote of Butterfly McQueen, "There is nobody to whom this lively, wise and skillful player can be compared. . . . She is a one-woman masterpiece.

"Hattie McDaniel, always so magnificent, plays Scarlett's nanny superbly.

"Special mention goes to Everett Brown as Big Sam. And a special welcome goes to Oscar Polk as Pork. Oscar Polk played the Angel Gabriel in the film version of *The Green Pastures*, and he gave the role, besides all the angelic virtues, added qualities as a sort of celestial Pullman porter. . . . This book *(GWTW)* provides him with such another role."

But these were Atlanta notices, and as such, basically small-town stuff. The bigger test would come four days later, on the glittering Great White Way—Broadway.

Because neither of the two MGM-affiliated theaters in the area was large enough to accommodate the intended audience, the New York premiere was held simultaneously at both of them, the Astor on Times Square and the Capitol, a few blocks away.

The evening of December 19. Light spilled out over the crowd in flashing neon and moving electric bulbs that spelled out *GWTW* in huge, bright letters. The heady aroma of coffee from the doughnut shops on either side of the Astor mingled with the scents of perfume and furs and exhaust fumes from the sleek, swank Lincolns and Cadillacs from which the cream of New York society emerged to enter the theater.

Socialites dripping with jewels and corseted in mink and ermine wafted into the theater on the arms of expensive escorts in top hats and tails.

Downtown, Gimbel's Department Store's windows were draped with Belle Watling's gown, Scarlett's white ruffled dress, Ashley's Confederate uniform, and Rhett's evening suit.

At the Capitol, usherettes in antebellum costume handed out programs in a lobby massed with gladiolas and decorated with huge portraits of Scarlett and Rhett.

Jimmy Stewart squired Olivia de Havilland. Barbara O'Neil arrived with her husband, Broadway producer Joshua Logan. Mr. Frederics, a famous hat designer who got screen credit for Scarlett's bonnets, was on hand, although his contributions seem to have been replaced by Walter Plunkett's. Alice Faye, Tony Martin, Ann Rutherford, and Walter Winchell also appeared at the Capitol's.

The last limo pulled away from the curb. At both theaters, the houselights dimmed, the curtain went up, and *Gone With the Wind* faced a new set of notices.

As in Atlanta, the audiences loved the film. So did the critics, although New York's writers, having to support their sophisticated reputation, mixed a tad of cynicism in with the kudos.

Kate Cameron of the New York *Daily News* suggested that "one must be feeling hale and hearty to stand the strain of the long sitting . . . but for those who can bear it, *GWTW* is worth every moment of that time."

The New York Times critic, granting that *Gone With the Wind* was "a great show," also noted: " . . . we still feel that color is hard on the eyes for so long a picture."

(Continued on page 236)

A list of The Players and The Staff as shown in the motion picture tie-in edition of the novel.

THE PLAYERS

IN THE ORDER OF THEIR APPEARANCE

AT TARA, THE O'HARA PLANTATION IN GEORGIA

BRENT TARLETON	Fred Crane
STUART TARLETON	George Reeves
SCARLETT O'HARA	Vivien Leigh
MAMMY	Hattie McDaniel
BIG SAM	Everett Brown
ELIJAH	Zack Williams
GERALD O'HARA	Thomas Mitchell
PORK	Oscar Polk
ELLEN O'HARA	Barbara O'Neil
JONAS WILKERSON	Victor Jory
SUELLEN O'HARA	Evelyn Keyes
CARREEN O'HARA	Ann Rutherford
PRISSY	Butterfly McQueen

AT TWELVE OAKS, THE NEARBY WILKES PLANTATION

JOHN WILKES	Howard Hickman
INDIA WILKES	Alicia Rhett
ASHLEY WILKES	Leslie Howard
MELANIE HAMILTON	Olivia de Havilland
CHARLES HAMILTON	Rand Brooks
FRANK KENNEDY	Carroll Nye
CATHLEEN CALVERT	Marcella Martin
RHETT BUTLER	Clark Gable

AT THE BAZAAR IN ATLANTA

AUNT "PITTYPAT" HAMILTON	Laura Hope Crews
DOCTOR MEADE	Harry Davenport
MRS. MEADE	Leona Roberts
MRS. MERRIWETHER	Jane Darwell
RENÉ PICARD	Albert Morin
MAYBELLE MERRIWETHER	Mary Anderson
FANNY ELSING	Terry Shero
OLD LEVI	William McClain

IN AUNT "PITTYPAT'S" HOME

UNCLE PETER	Eddie Anderson

OUTSIDE THE EXAMINER OFFICE

PHIL MEADE	Jackie Moran

AT THE HOSPITAL

Reminiscent soldier	Cliff Edwards
BELLE WATLING	Ona Munson
The Sergeant	Ed Chandler
A wounded soldier	George Hackathorne
A convalescent soldier	Roscoe Ates
A dying soldier	John Arledge
An amputation case	Eric Linden

DURING THE EVACUATION

A commanding officer	Tom Tyler

DURING THE SIEGE

A mounted officer	William Bakewell
The Bartender	Lee Phelps

GEORGIA AFTER SHERMAN

The Yankee Deserter	Paul Hurst
The Carpetbagger's friend	Ernest Whitman
A returning veteran	William Stelling
A hungry soldier	Louis Jean Heydt
EMMY SLATTERY	Isabel Jewell

DURING RECONSTRUCTION

The Yankee Major	Robert Elliott
His poker-playing captains	George Meeker / Wallis Clark
The Corporal	Irving Bacon
A Carpetbagger orator	Adrian Morris
JOHNNY GALLEGHER	J. M. Kerrigan
A Carpetbagger business man	Olin Howland
A renegade	Yakima Canutt
His companion	Blue Washington
TOM, a Yankee captain	Ward Bond
BONNIE BLUE BUTLER	Cammie King
BEAU WILKES	Mickey Kuhn
Bonnie's nurse	Lillian Kemble Cooper

THE STAFF

The Production designed by	WILLIAM CAMERON MENZIES
Art direction by	LYLE WHEELER
Photographed by	ERNEST HALLER, A.S.C.
Technicolor Associates	{ RAY RENNAHAN, A.S.C. { WILFRID M. CLINE, A.S.C.
Musical score by	MAX STEINER
Associate	LOU FORBES
Special Photographic effects by	JACK COSGROVE
Associate: Fire effects	LEE ZAVITZ
Costumes designed by	WALTER PLUNKETT
Scarlett's hats by	JOHN FREDERICS
Interiors by	JOSEPH B. PLATT
Interior decoration by	EDWARD G. BOYLE
Supervising Film Editor	HAL C. KERN
Associate Film Editor	JAMES E. NEWCOM
Scenario Assistant	BARBARA KEON
Recorder	FRANK MAHER
Makeup and hair styling	MONTY WESTMORE
Associates	{ HAZEL ROGERS { BEN NYE
Dance Directors	{ FRANK FLOYD { EDDIE PRINZ

Historian	WILBUR G. KURTZ
Technical Advisers	{ SUSAN MYRICK { WILL PRICE
Research	LILLIAN K. DEIGHTON

Production Manager	RAYMOND A. KLUNE
Technicolor Co. Supervision	NATALIE KALMUS
Associate	HENRI JAFFA
Assistant Director	ERIC G. STACEY
Second Assistant Director	RIDGEWAY CALLOW
Production continuity	{ LYDIA SCHILLER { CONNIE EARLE

Mechanical Engineer	R. D. MUSGRAVE
Construction Superintendent	HAROLD FENTON
Chief Grip	FRED WILLIAMS
In charge of Wardrobe	EDWARD P. LAMBERT
Associates	{ MARIAN DABNEY { ELMER ELLSWORTH

Casting Managers	{ CHARLES RICHARDS { FRED SCHUESSLER
Location Manager	MASON LITSON
Scenic Department Superintendent	HENRY J. STAHL
Electrical Superintendent	WALLY OETTEL
Chief Electrician	JAMES POTEVIN
Properties:	
Manager	HAROLD COLES
On the set	ARDEN CRIPE
Greens	ROY A. McLAUGHLIN
Drapes	JAMES FORNEY
Special properties made by	ROSS B. JACKMAN
Tara landscaped by	FLORENCE YOCK
Still Photographer	FRED PARRISH
Camera Operators	{ ARTHUR ARLING { VINCENT FARRAR
Assistant Film Editors	{ RICHARD VAN ENGER { ERNEST LEADLEY

A call sheet for the location sequence in Tara's vegetable garden. In this scene, where Scarlett gags on a radish, Vivien Leigh refused to make the required wretching noises, so Olivia de Havilland dubbed them in for her later.

SELZNICK INTERNATIONAL PICTURES, INC.
CALL SHEET

DATE __TUES., MAY 23, 1939__

PICTURE __"GONE WITH THE WIND"__ PROD. NO. __108__ DIRECTOR: __VICTOR FLEMING__

SET __EXT. TARA – VEGETABLE GARDEN__ __SUMMER 1864 (WEATHER PERM.)__

LOCATION __OLD LASKY MESA__ SET NO. __2__ SCENES __Sc. 383 (DAWN)__

NAME	TIME CALLED		CHARACTER, DESC., WARDROBE
	ON SET Lv.Studio	MAKE-UP	
Vivien Leigh	2:00 AM	1:00 AM	Scarlett #11A
Stand-in	2:00 AM	1:30 AM	For Miss Leigh

L A T E R

EXT.TARA-CREEK BOTTOM COTTON PATCH & EXT.COVERED WAY-SCS.398 to 407,432

AUTUMN 1864

Vivien Leigh	--	--	Scarlett #12
Thomas Mitchell	5:00 AM	3:00 AM	Gerald #5
Hattie McDaniel	5:00 AM	4:30 AM	Mammy #5
Butterfly McQueen	5:00 AM	4:30 AM	Prissy #7
Evelyn Keyes	5:00 AM	3:00 AM	Suellen #4
Ann Rutherford	5:00 AM	3:00 AM	Careen #4
Oscar Polk	5:00 AM	4:30 AM	Pork #5A

L A T E R

EXT.TARA (THROUGH 2ND STORY WINDOW) - SC. 431 - AUTUMN 1864 (Yankee Cavalry Seq.)

Olivia de Havilland	8:30 AM	(pickup)	Melanie #7
Thomas Mitchell	-	-	Gerald #5
Evelyn Keyes	-	-	Suellen #4
Ann Rutherford	-	-	Careen #4
Stand-in	8:30 AM	(pickup)	For Miss de Havilland

TRANSPORTATION

CAMERAS (Ready) - - -	3:30 AM		Bus (Crew) leave	1:00 AM
SOUND (Ready) - - - -	4:00 AM		Staff cars "	2:00 AM
P.A.SYSTEM (Ready) -	3:30 AM		Miss Leigh's car lvs.	2:00 AM
WIND MACHINE (Ready) -	4:00 AM		Trucks leave	12:45 AM
			Balance of transp.	5:00 AM
BREAKFAST (Ready) - -	5:00 AM			
LUNCH (Ready) - - - -	11:00 AM		PROPERTY DEPT.	
			Cow on location	6:30 AM

ADVANCE SHOOTING SCHEDULE
ON REVERSE SIDE OF CALL SHEET

ASSISTANT DIRECTOR __ERIC STACEY__

ADVANCE SHOOTING SCHEDULE

Wednesday, May 24	-	Int. Scarlett's Bedroom (Continuation)	Stage #11
Thursday, May 25	-	Int. Dining Room & Hall (Row & Rape Seq.)	Stage #14
Friday, May 26	-	Int. Rhett's House (Rhett's return & miscarriage seq.)	Stage #14
Saturday, May 27	-	Int. Rhett's House (Death of Bonnie Seq.)	Stage #11
Monday, May 29	-	Int. Rhett's House (Rhett-Melanie Sc. re: Bonnie's burial)	Stage #14

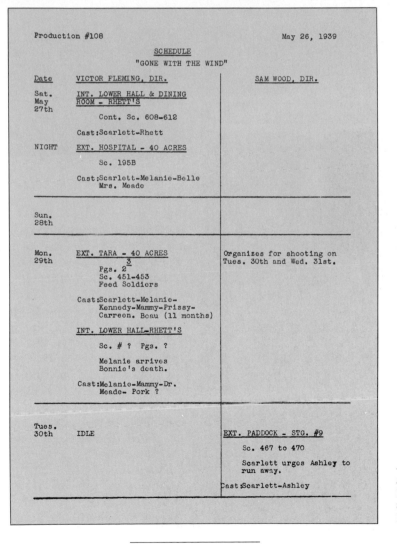

Production #108   May 26, 1939

SCHEDULE
"GONE WITH THE WIND"

Date	VICTOR FLEMING, DIR.	SAM WOOD, DIR.
Sat. May 27th	INT. LOWER HALL & DINING ROOM - RHETT'S Cont. Sc. 608-612 Cast:Scarlett-Rhett	
NIGHT	EXT. HOSPITAL - 40 ACRES Sc. 195B Cast:Scarlett-Melanie-Belle Mrs. Meade	
Sun. 28th		
Mon. 29th	EXT. TARA - 40 ACRES 3 Pgs. 2 Sc. 451-453 Feed Soldiers Cast:Scarlett-Melanie-Kennedy-Mammy-Prissy-Carreen. Beau (11 months) INT. LOWER HALL-RHETT'S Sc. # ? Pgs. ? Melanie arrives Bonnie's death. Cast:Melanie-Mammy-Dr. Meade- Pork ?	Organizes for shooting on Tues. 30th and Wed. 31st.
Tues. 30th	IDLE	EXT. PADDOCK - STG. #9 Sc. 467 to 470 Scarlett urges Ashley to run away. Cast:Scarlett-Ashley

A mimeographed production schedule for May 26, 1939.

Wilbur Kurtz, production historian, poses with the painting he did on commission for Georgia's Governor Rivers. The building is the old Governor's Mansion; the figure on horseback is Leslie Howard as Ashley Wilkes.

An original one-sheet poster (27″ x 41″), used in theaters around the nation during 1939 and 1940.

(Continued from page 231)

The newspaper went on to vote it one of the ten best films of 1939.

Now all that remained was the last great hurdle before general release: the Hollywood premiere.

Thursday, December 28. Ten thousand cheering fans jammed San Vicente Boulevard and the walkway to the Carthay Circle Theater. Bathed in the brilliant glow of massed searchlights, the jewels of America's entertainment industry swept into the theater on a tidal wave of sheer glamour, a moviegoer's dream come true.

Here in all their glory were all the luminous stars of Hollywood, including: Carole Lombard, draped in gold lamé, linked with the suave Mr. Gable; Vivien Leigh and the dashing Larry Olivier; Ginger Rogers, resplendent in gown and turban designed by Walter Plunkett; William Powell, Orson Welles, Ann Southern, Ann Sheridan, Fred

An insert poster (14″ x 36″), used in theater lobbies to promote the film. When the movie was released at regular prices in 1941, a gummed label was attached, which declared, "Nothing Cut But The Price."

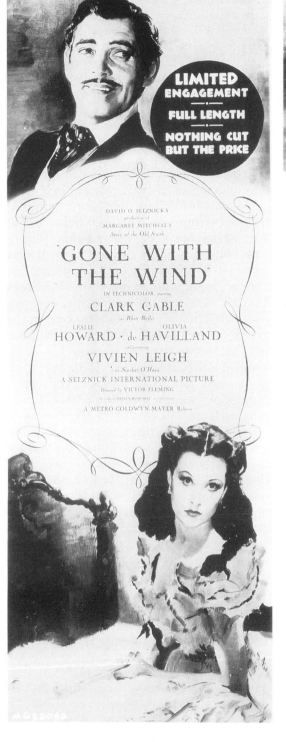

Another one-sheet poster used to advertise the film in 1939 and 1940.

A three-sheet (41″ x 79″) advertising poster, which was often displayed on billboards during 1939 and 1940.

MacMurray, Fanny Brice, Claudette Colbert, Hedy Lamarr, Mr. and Mrs. Temple with Shirley, Mr. and Mrs. Harpo Marx...the list ran on and on.

Everyone who had been in *GWTW*—or who had vied for and cried for parts—was at the premiere. And once again, the film worked its magic.

This was borne out at the Academy Awards presentation in February 1940, as *GWTW* swept away with a record ten Oscars.

Besides wresting away the Best Picture award from Victor Fleming's other gem of 1939, *The Wizard of Oz*, there were accolades for Vivien Leigh as Best Actress and Hattie McDaniel as Best Supporting Actress. This was the first Oscar to be awarded to a Black performer.

To the surprise of many, Clark Gable lost out to Robert Donat in *Goodbye, Mr. Chips* for the honor of Best Actor, and Thomas Mitchell won Best Supporting Actor, not for his lilting Gerald O'Hara but for his work in *Stagecoach* with John Wayne.

But Victor Fleming, competing against the formidable Frank Capra for *Mr. Smith Goes to Washington*, and *GWTW*'s own unacknowledged Sam Wood for *Goodbye, Mr. Chips*, walked off with Best Director.

Sidney Howard posthumously received an Oscar for Best Screenplay, winning out over Ben Hecht (of the grueling week's rewrite) and Charles MacArthur for *Wuthering Heights*.

Cinematography and film editing Oscars went, respectively, to Ernest Haller and Ray Rennahan, and to Hal Kern and James Newcom, with Art Direction and Special Effects awards for Lyle Wheeler and Jack Cosgrove.

William Cameron Menzies was presented with a special award for Outstanding Achievement in the Use of Color, while David Selznick received the Irving Thalberg Memorial Award for Most Consistent High Level of Production Achievement by an Individual Producer. This had particular significance for Selznick, as he and the late Mr. Thalberg had been friends and colleagues for years.

The Academy Awards were granted, the gala premieres over and done. But *Gone With the Wind* did not sail off into the sunset, never to be heard from again, nor fade into a gentle oblivion like so many other thirties films. Instead it became a phenomenon, a legend, growing stronger with every passing year.

From the first it was honored with anniversary festivals like a lovingly indulged princess.

Loew's Grand was the host of the 1940 "premiere," which was to have been presided over by Vivien Leigh and Laurence Olivier (with proceeds going to the British War Relief Society). But Mother Nature took the reins. The Atlanta airport was fogged in solid. Vivien and Larry were unable to land, and camera-shy Margaret Mitchell was left to conduct the ceremonies single-handedly, with no one but a newly named and inexperienced Miss GWTW Anniversary for backup.

During this time *Gone With the Wind* went into general release. Audiences throughout America could see it at prices ranging from 75 cents to $1.10 per seat.

David Selznick threw himself into the advertising and distribution of the picture as fervently as he had overseen everything else connected with it. He had once even issued a directive to Howard Dietz regarding the type of paper to be used in the programs for the film. "Sometimes their crackling noise makes it difficult to hear the dialogue. Promise you will attend to this."

Selznick felt that audiences who came to see *GWTW* were expecting a treat, a special evening of movie magic, and he was determined to give it to them. He personally conducted surveys to ascertain whether the intermission was long enough, whether patrons were happier with reserved or open seats, and how people felt about the higher than normal prices.

At his instigation, a twelve-page booklet, "Suggestions for Presentation of *Gone With the Wind*," was sent to theater owners

This easel-backed photo art card (16" x 22") was used to advertise the film in 1939 and 1940. You can see that the painting of Rhett and Scarlett has been derived from one of Clarence Bull's portrait photographs.

along with the film, bearing tips on everything from when to dim the houselights and start the music to how many minutes to allow for the intermission to when to dip the final curtain.

Selznick also directed MGM's publicity push to its various branch offices. A strict list of guidelines included such ordinances as: "DON'T call this a Metro-Goldwyn-Mayer picture. It is a Selznick International Picture. DON'T write publicity stories about Margaret Mitchell. DON'T refer to the Tarletons...as 'the Tarleton twins.' They should be called either 'the Tarleton boys' or 'the Tarleton brothers.' *And most importantly*, DON'T refer to the BURNING OF ATLANTA as such. The scene in the pic-

ture is *not* the burning of Atlanta but rather the burning of certain buildings containing war materials."

Whatever it was called, the picture swept like wildfire across the country, with MGM heralding it as "The Greatest Motion Picture Ever Made."

Audiences apparently agreed, as *GWTW* collected awards for several years running. In 1939, *Photoplay* magazine gave its Tiffany gold medal to David Selznick for his work on the film. In 1940, the National Board of Review praised it as One of the Ten Best Pictures of the Year, and in 1941 *The Film Daily* prized it as Best Picture of that year. The movie's domino-effect distribution schedule across the country made it eligible for these awards three years in a row.

Its continuing popularity was a boon to marketers, and a rich panoply of tie-in merchandise has followed it over the years.

There were leather buttons shaped like books and embossed with the title (used to promote the novel in the thirties); Rhett and Scarlett cast-iron bookends; lockets; chocolates; and hair bows. Rhett Butler bow ties and Scarlett-style cameo brooches made of tin (just send in fifteen cents and three Lux soap wrappers). You could buy Scarlett perfume (in Apple Blossom or Bittersweet), Scarlett nail polish (in shades of Night, Morning, and Noon), and seeds for Scarlett O'Hara morning glories.

The movie-struck consumer could purchase *Gone With the Wind* dolls and paper dolls, cookbooks, watercolor paint books, china figurines, cotton hankies, jigsaw puzzles and games, dress patterns and dresses, rayon print fabric and straw bonnets, snoods and neckties and linen kitchen calendars. And the list continues with cigarette rollers, playing cards (the aces carried a picture of Rhett playing poker in the Yankee jail), collector plates, a seat on the Gray Line bus company's GWTW Pilgrimage Tour, and a postage stamp from the Fiji Islands, all commemorating the film.

When the Loew's Grand was torn down in the late sixties to make way for an office complex, people gladly bought the bricks from its skeleton and squares of carpet from the lobby. This did not, however, signal the end of an era. *Gone With the Wind* was still going strong.

The book was still widely read, not only in America but also throughout the world. Banned by the Nazis during World War II, it was passed from hand to hand along the French Underground. Oppressed people rallied to Scarlett's courage and fortitude in the face of a similar oppression. In bombed and blitzed London, crowds queued in patient lines to see the film. And in America, the movie, barely cold from its premiere showings, was reissued in 1942 as a boost to wartime moral.

It was reissued again in 1947, and following an MGM master plan, at roughly seven-year intervals thereafter. Although MGM had leased most of its old films to television stations, it vowed that neither *GWTW* nor *The Wizard of Oz* would receive such cavalier treatment. They would be shown only in theaters or by television networks under special circumstances.

Ted Turner's purchase of the MGM library some forty years later has turned back the clock. Once again one can catch daily showings of *Gone With the Wind*, this time at Turner's CNN Center in Atlanta.

Those not conveniently located to Atlanta can see it on their home VCRs, for the videotape is widely carried at video sales and rental outlets and even local libraries.

Before the advent of the VCR, the film was shown once on national television in 1976, and before that, between 1967 and 1973, various musical stage versions were presented in Tokyo, London, Los Angeles, and San Francisco. The Japanese version—there were actually three—was by far the most popular and ran, in its third incarnation, a lengthy six hours. The London and U.S. shows were not well received and fizzled shortly after their debuts.

But these forays into backstage bathos in no way diminished the story's popularity. It is regenerated with constant discoveries by new viewers and readers, and every time its words and images are replayed to those who have seen it before.

Almost from the moment it hit the bookstands in 1936, readers have been clamoring for a sequel. Margaret Mitchell steadfastly refused to write one, insisting that, for her, the story had ended exactly where she left it. She didn't know if Scarlett ever got Rhett back, and apparently she didn't care. She was killed by a drunk driver in August 1949—at age 48—without ever changing her mind.

Her death has been often imbued with an aura of mystery. The most mystifying aspect, though, is why the man who hit her, with twenty-three prior drunk driving con-

(Continued on page 244)

This cardboard window card (14″ x 22″) was used to promote the film in 1939 and 1940.

A large framed display (30″ x 72″) such as this was sometimes used in theater lobbies in 1939 and 1940.

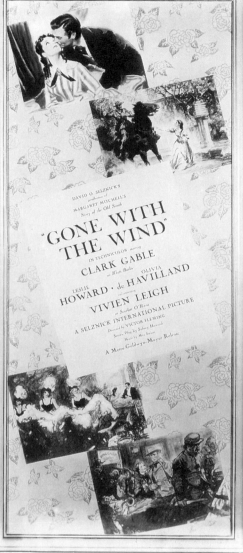

"Scarlett" cologne, produced by Pinaud of New York City in 1939

A *GWTW* paper doll book put out by the Merrill Publishing Company of Chicago in 1940. Notice the presence of Wade Hamilton, Scarlett's son, who doesn't exist in the movie.

The front and back covers of the movie program. You could buy it for 25 cents in theaters where the film was playing on road-show release.

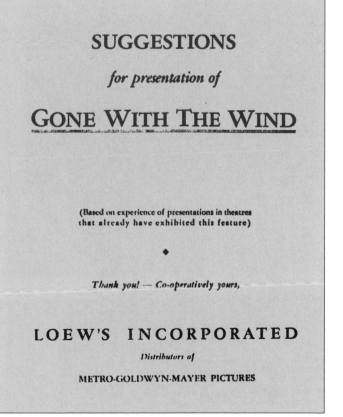

In this 12-page booklet, David Selznick offered to-the-letter instructions to theater managers for presentation of his studio's film epic.

(Continued from page 240)
victions, was still behind the wheel.

On the evening of the disastrous collision, Margaret and her husband, John, had gone out to see a movie. Parking across the street from the theater, they were less than halfway across the tarmac when the careening car appeared, bearing straight at them. Margaret, supporting John—weak from a lingering heart condition—stepped back toward the curb, while John apparently moved forward. The driver, presumably anticipating the husband's actions rather than the wife's, hit her. Six days later she was dead.

Leslie Howard had gone before her into the world beyond, and his death, too, carried a hint of mystery. He was on an aircraft bound for England from Gibraltar in May 1943, when it was shot down by the Germans. It was speculated that either they thought Churchill was aboard, or they knew the actor was on a secret intelligence mission for the Allies.

Despite accidents, acts of war, and the endless march of time, *Gone With the Wind* lives on, preserving the glorious talents of Margaret Mitchell and Leslie Howard, David Selznick and Vivien Leigh, Clark Gable and Olivia de Havilland, Thomas Mitchell, Barbara O'Neil, Hattie McDaniel, Butterfly McQueen and Oscar Polk, Cukor and Fleming, Sam Wood and Sidney Howard, and everyone of the 4,400 people involved in the making of the movie.

GWTW shines as clearly today as it did when it was made. It is a tribute to drama, spectacle, and color; to spunk and fire and determination; to courage, conviction, and daring to put heart and soul into something you believe in.

It speaks to people on a subconscious level that is sometimes difficult to define. But it sparks the imagination and the spirit. And as long as there are audiences , *Gone With the Wind* will live on.

ABOUT THE AUTHORS

Herb Bridges is the world's leading authority on *Gone With the Wind* and has amassed the world's largest collection of *GWTW* memorabilia. Along with Terryl C. Boodman, he is co-editor of *Gone With the Wind: The Screenplay*. He has published three other books about the movie, *The Filming of Gone With the Wind, Frankly, My Dear . . .*, and *Scarlet Fever*. He lives in Atlanta, Georgia.

Terryl C. Boodman, a writer and long-time fan of GWTW, is the co-author of *China Through the Eyes of a Tiger* with Roland Sperry and co-editor of *Gone With the Wind: The Screenplay*. She lives in Orange County, California.